WHAT NOT TO DO IN COLLEGE

BUT YOU PROBABLY WILL

D. BEIRNE

This book is dedicated to all of the
people who know college tuition is really
just a $250,000 cover charge. Woo!

Table of Contents

Table of Contents

Dear Reader,

Good for you for deciding to read this book. I'm proud of you! This may be the best decision you make in your entire college career...... seriously.

So here's what you're about to get involved in: a journey that will take you through the truth of college life by suggesting some things you shouldn't do. That journey will be very superficial and also a pretty good time. Full disclosure: these are all things that people have done and will probably still do until all colleges implode.

It's survival of the fittest, my friends. Use this book as your lifeline, your cheat sheet, your get-out-of-jail-free card (literally). Have some fun and good luck. You'll need it.

D.B.

101:

Don't Skip Class

You know what you have a ton of in college? **FREEDOM!** Finally, you're there, you're on campus, you're hanging out with new people, you're eating what you want when you want, you're showering on your own terms, you're wearing cropped tops with wild abandon, you're figuring out where you'll put your first tattoo, which, by the way, will probably be terrible. You're totally doing you and that's awesome. Congrats on being you.

The undying quest for freedom is the reason you've been dislocating your eyeballs since birth every time your parents told you what to do—seriously, there are GIFs of babies eye rolling and every one of them is hilarious. For eighteen years you've been *patiently* waiting for freedom while you were burdened by someone else doing your laundry, cooking your meals, keeping you alive, and paying for all your shit. You poor thing <insert baby eye roll here>. But alas, now you have it. College equals freedom. *Sweet, sweet freedom.* The one thing you're gonna want to remember, though, is that your original intention was actually to go to college to get a degree.

Blah, blah, blah college degree, right we get it. WOOO BURRITOS AT 2AM! But it's true, you're there for a purpose beyond finding out how many keg stands you can do and how you can increase your "number" (that's a reference to sexual partners, if you didn't get it then you're probably not actively trying to *increase your number*). This means that you will actually have to go to class. Hey man, I get it, it's super easy to *not* go to class, but probably not the best idea in the grand scheme of things.

Here are some situations you may find yourself in that might make you choose not to go to class:

- You're hungover
- It's raining, snowing, really nice, too hot, or too cold out—so basically there's weather outside
- It's Monday
- You have a test and didn't study
- You're really comfortable in your bed
- You're really comfortable in some-one else's bed
- Someone may have told you class was cancelled but maybe they said not cancelled, you can't be too sure so you play it safe and assume they said "cancelled"
- It's Friday

- You can't pause your video game because you'll mess up your score
- You woke up and had no idea where you were
- They're serving something good in the dining hall and you don't want to risk missing it by being in class
- The show you're binge watching is at a really pivotal part
- It's any day of the week

Sure these are all great reasons to skip class, but you should probably try to rally and make the effort. Think of it this way—you or your parents or a bank (which means you in four years) are paying loads of money for that college degree. Literally mortgage level money, like four really-nice-cars-level money, a commercial-flight-to-space-level money (in 75 years when the prices are reduced by nine million dollars). So, if you don't go to class you're essentially throwing houses, cars and a trip to space right down the toilet along with the 12 beers you drank way too fast last Tuesday afternoon when you weren't in class. Ummmm, don't do that Mr. or Mrs. Monopoly.

Consider going to class to be your job. If you do this job well, then, in the end, you'll probably get another pretty decent job or the ability to keep going to college.

Here's something you should know—college professors know the people who go to their classes and the people who don't, and when it comes time to submit their grades, they tend to *like* the kids who've made the effort to go to class. This can make the difference between an A and an A-, or if it's a class like Western Civ, the difference between a C and a D. There's only like 12-15 hours **A WEEK** that you'll even *have* class, which means you can put that kind of time in. So wake up and go to class, dumbasses, like it's your freakin' job!

Oh, and when you're parents come up for Parent's Weekend try to steer them away from the professor who's class you've been avoiding, or an awkward conversation may ensue like one where your parents say, "Yeah, my diligent, studious daughter said she is having such a hard time in your class," and your professor responds with something like, "I've never seen your daughter before in my life." Oops.

102:

Don't Forget to Wash Your Sheets

You know what's really gross? **Dirty-ass sheets.** Those things you sleep on every night, drooling on, excreting some other kinds of bodily fluids on. Those things you put your filthy feet into after walking around the floor you haven't vacuumed in nine weeks. Those things you've been rolling around on with God only knows who/what. Those things that are the only line of protection between you and the jailhouse filth mattress you're sleeping on. Yeah, those things need to get washed.

Imagine bringing someone back to your dorm to roll around on those sheets and the first words out of their mouth are, "What's that smell?"

Imagine sitting on your bed for seven hours watching Netflix then getting up to go to the dining hall only to discover, by someone else pointing it out, that you have a lollipop, a glow stick and a condom wrapper stuck to your back.

Imagine yourself thinking twice before using your sheets as a tourniquet to save your best friend's life because you're pretty sure your nasty sheets could make their life threatening artery-laceration **waaaaay** worse. Uh, no.

If you start noticing a funky smell on your bed, or worse, on your body when you wake up in the morning…. or afternoon, you've waited too long. If you see white spots on your groovy navy blue sheets that you can't account for, you've waited to long. If there is more popcorn under your covers than in the 28-gallon, three-flavor tin your old neighbor sent you, you've waited too long. If your friends actively choose to stand rather than sit on your bed to play Xbox, you've waited too long. If you can't remember the last time you washed your sheets, then you have waited **too daggone long**.

So wash your sheets, you filthy animal, and stop being so gross! And BTW, if your bath towel is so stiff that it can stand up on its own, if it started out white and now is some shade of grey, green or orange, throw it in with the sheets. And also…**you're gross**.

103:

Don't Leave Your Dishes In The Sink

Now here's the thing—I don't want you to think by the title that I'm unreasonable. When I say *don't leave your dishes in the sink* I mean don't leave your dishes in the sink for more than two days. Listen, we all know when we're making a box of mac-n-cheese at 3AM that nobody's doing the dishes. **That's crazy and maybe a little bit inhumane.** But, if your dishes are sitting in the sink, or the floor or your bed, two days later, you're gonna need to step up, get the soap out, and start scrubbing.

You might think this only applies to you if you live in a house or apartment, but let me assure you, my dorm residing friends, this applies to you too. A sink full of neon green plastic dishes from Target caked with dried Ramen noodles and baked beans is scientifically proven to make a hangover 13x worse. There's absolutely no science to back that statement up, but I feel like it's still probably true. And when you leave your plastic dishes with food in them for more than a day or two, they start to develop an odor that even your grandmother can't get out, no matter how many of her old school voodoo tricks she tries... using weird things like vinegar, the bark of a tree and something grey she keeps in a plastic bag under her sink.

You have those dishes for a reason—to hold your food. Do you have other options when your dishes are dirty? Sure. You have your roommate's dishes, a couple of strategically-placed paper towels, an ashtray, your sociology textbook. But really, even these clever replacements will not hold up to the unique pallet you develop in college or the ketchup you think pairs well with pizza bites (it doesn't). And eventually you'll need those dishes.

The solution to your dish problem is very simple. Wash your damn dishes. Or get a sleeve of 350 disposable ones from a box store and proudly contribute to the straight up murder of the planet. Either way.

FYI, it's super annoying for the people that live with you to have to deal with your dirty dishes. So be courteous to your roommates, housemates or dormmates, and get your damn dishes out of sink. Also, it's an unwritten but totally reasonable rule to pile your housemate's dishes in their bed if they have left them in the sink too freakin' long. You've been warned.

104:

Don't Do Hard Drugs

There are so many things that you *can* and *will* do in college and **good for you, make memories, have a blast**. Try out a new hairstyle; break out the buzzer and purple dye! Try a new look, bring back hippies....again! Try out a new music genre, introduce yourself to Pink Floyd! Do all of these things because they're awesome and when *your* kids go to college you'll have at least one story that you can actually share with them when they think their new nose ring is the craziest thing ever. But of the things you will do, it's better if you **don't do hard drugs**.

If you're thinking that hard drugs would be hard to find for a regular schmo like yourself then you are probably not smart enough to go to college or read this book, and this book is very **not smart**. Believe me, they'll be there and you'll know people who do them, buy them, and sell them. But don't be one of those people.

Trust me, the girl I went to school with who took a walk out of her *second floor* dorm room window and broke her pelvis probably wishes she stayed away from those hard drugs she was *just gonna try one time*. That guy that I know who died, was brought back to life, and spent a year in rehab at age 20 just to get himself to the point of being able to walk up four steps again, probably wishes he laid off the hard shit. You may think you're smart and know how your body will react but you're not that smart, because you definitely would not be reading this if you were. You may think you have enough body weight to balance out the pills you pop but that's not the way that works. You might think that since your friends didn't die that you wouldn't either—ever hear of **Russian Roulette**? Bottom line is you have no idea what will happen to you if you take hard drugs and the odds are really not in anyone's favor.

And this isn't to scare you into thinking that you could die or have serious physical injuries like a broken pelvis, ruptured breast implants, or a dislocated face. You are also in legit jeopardy of looking like a straight up asshole. When someone I went to school with stumbled home one morning after tripping on acid all night long and suddenly proclaimed that she had a profound epiphany and would "never use the word *seriously* again", you know what I was thinking? *Asshole*. BTW, within 20 minutes after arriving home she was using the word *seriously* to an almost offensive degree. Asshole.

So stay away from the pharmaceuticals un-prescribed to you and the shit someone concocted in a dirty cement basement and the cocaine because this isn't 1980's Wall Street. You'll have a slightly better chance of surviving college and not looking like a total asshole if you do.

105:

Don't Pee In Your Closet

Hahaha this won't be me, you're thinking. I don't even know anyone that this would apply to, you're thinking. Let me assure you, if you are thinking either one of those things then you haven't been to college yet. Or if you have been to college and still think either one of those things then **you must've commuted**.

You might start out freshman year thinking you're gonna do amazing things like travel and get good grades and volunteer at a homeless shelter and only party on Saturday nights with a delicate white wine, and good for you if you do, more power to you. But you should know it is *possible* that one morning senior year, you wake up naked with your boyfriend sleeping on the floor and when you ask why he is sleeping on the floor, there is a chance he might inform you that he has chosen to distance himself from your body because in the middle of the night you got up and **peed in your closet**. I'm not saying that this is a likely event but it is probably more possible than you realize.

This fragile bladder problem tends to have a direct correlation to alcohol consumption. Or we can call it like it is and say it pretty much only happens when you are **balls-out hammered**. As a matter of a fact, if this happens when you're not wildly intoxicated then you need to see a urologist. An *over-abundance* of alcohol consumption makes peeing in your closet far more likely than an *under-abundance* of alcohol consumption, though I'm not sure that an *under-abundance* exists in college so there's really no point in even offering it up as a possibility.

Maybe you think that if you don't have a closet in your room you won't have to worry about this one, and it's true, you don't have to worry about peeing in your closet because, as we have just established, you don't have a closet. **In that case, here are some other places that you should consider not urinating in or on:**

- The living room floor of your off-campus house
- Your RA's door
- The campus security booth
- The stairwell in your dorm
- The college president's front door
- A passing child
- The stacks in the library
- Your roommate's sound system
- In a cop car
- On a cop car
- On a cop

There are many other places that you shouldn't urinate, but maybe make it easy on yourself and instead of thinking about where you *shouldn't* urinate, consider where you *should*. The toilet. And maybe a bush. That list is much easier to remember. I should point out that when I heard the story of a friend having gotten up in the middle of the night after crashing in the bed of another friend and peeing on the shag carpet right in the middle of the room, I thought, no way, impossible. But when I went to investigate the alleged crime and saw the large wet spot in the middle of the rug and lifted the blanket under which my friend still slept only to be blinded by her big, white ass because she couldn't get her pants back up, I realized that said story was, in fact, true.

So in order to avoid something super devastating like standing up next to the bed your sweet girlfriend is sleeping on and peeing directly on her actual head, please empty your bladder before you go to bed, regardless of the state you're in, and make sure that you're peeing in a toilet… not the vegetable drawer of the refrigerator. Oh and if you happen to be sleeping on your friend's couch and you pee on that, at least have the decency to flip the cushion over in the morning and **NEVER** tell them what's on the other side.

106:

Don't Post Dumb Shit On Social Media

You know what's awesome? **College**. You know what's not awesome? Waking up to a voicemail from your mom telling you that when she was at church she heard about the Slapclap (aka Snapchat) video of her sweet angel chugging cheap champagne in a bathroom with two girls wearing only short-shorts and bras. If you're smart enough to go to college then you're smart enough to know that if you post something on the Internet it stays on the Internet.

C'mon, do you really think that just because your account is private or that things allegedly *delete* after viewing or within 24 hours that actually means they can't be viewed by anyone? No, dummy, someone way smarter than you sitting in a dark room with twelve empty bottles of Red Bull and Mountain Dew scattered around the AstroTurf they use as a carpet can find them.

In case you're confused, here are some examples of things you shouldn't post on social media:

- Your boobs
- You doing a gravity bong hit
- You funneling an oversized funnel
- You puking after funneling an over-sized funnel
- Anything you do in/on the toilet
- Your peen
- You spray painting the local police station
- You smoking a blunt
- You freestyle rapping while intoxicated
- Your vag
- You chugging an entire bottle of cherry Burnett's
- You smoking a bowl
- You punching someone in the face (also don't punch people in the face)
- Your butt
- You in the act of stealing anything
- Any picture of you in real time while drunk, just wait to review those until sobriety sets in and then maybe post none of them

Go live your life for the experience you are having in the moment. Don't distract yourself from the experience by fixing your hair, pouting your lips, flexing your muscles and taking a pic so that some kid you went to elementary school with thinks you're having a great life… **JUST GO HAVE A GREAT LIFE**.

You might not be planning to run for Congress one day, you might not aspire to get a job at a great accounting firm in Manhattan, you might not want to be a teacher, you might not plan to ever be a parent, you might not hope to impress the parents of a person you like, but until you know for a **fact** that you will actually spend your whole adulthood living under the same rock as Patrick Star, don't post dumb shit on social media.

107:

Don't Get An STD

You know what **sucks**? Weird things leaking from your private parts. You know what doesn't suck? Not having weird things leaking from your private parts. Here's a tip on how to prevent an STD...**wear a freakin' condom!** Look, college is awesome and some of the things you might do in college are things you will never tell your children... or your parents... or a priest... or a judge, and **that's great**, but don't become the poster child for things you wish you did, like wearing a condom that time you went to Cancun for spring break and banged yourself right into a wiener-doctor's office with a jacked-up prostate.

We all know that you can find yourself in a moment that is super sexy and fun, and that moment might be spontaneous, but let's not make it regrettable by waking up three days later with **excruciating ball-pain and burning urination**. This is for guys **AND** girls—always be prepared with a condom of your own. It's not the other person's job to provide it. If you're comfortable enough to have sex then be confident enough to insist on protecting yourself.

Take care of your body, stand for something, be smart about the dumb shit you do. And if you do find yourself with something growing on your nether regions that wasn't there before, go to the doctor! Oh, BTW, that whole, *but it feels better without a condom* thing? Give me a break, you're young, it could be wrapped in steel wool and still feel good (NO IT WON'T, DON'T TRY THAT). So quit your whining, be grateful you're getting some, and **wrap it up!**

108:

Don't Do 21 Shots On Your 21st Birthday

Are you a two-ton walrus? No? Then why on earth would you think that doing 21 shots or having 21 drinks on your 21st birthday is a good idea? I don't care how much of a tolerance you've built up in your first two years of college…or whatever you may have been doing in high school… but let me assure you, Rockstar, *you ain't at 21-shot level*.

Turning 21 in college is literally **AWESOME**. You've been looking forward to this since you started applying for schools or since birth, who knows, I don't judge. You finally get to sell your fake ID to a freshman that resembles you or is at least the same gender, you finally don't have to worry about someone asking you to sign your name on a piece of paper three times to see if it matches up with the signature on your ID, you can drink a beer right in front of the cop at the end of the bar, all great things and *good for you*, HAPPY BIRTHDAY! But if you think you're gonna throw back 21 shots of tequila on your b'day, you know what it's not gonna be? A **happy** birthday.

So unless you're a sumo wrestler, a 900-pound farm animal, or an actual dump truck, reel it in and live to see another day. Go out, party and have your fun but be realistic. No one wants to scrape you up off the bar floor, your parents don't want to have to bail you out of jail, and getting your stomach pumped in the emergency room is way worse than *not* doing 21 shots on your 21st birthday…trust me.

109:

Don't Get Caught Hooking Up With Your Roommate's Ex

Hey man, I know that your roommate's ex can look pretty sexy at 2AM. I get it, a lot of people look sexy at 2AM. Let's be real, a lamppost and some Chex Mix can look sexy at 2AM. But by some miracle, 2AM is often followed by **the next day** and in the light of that **next day**, some of your 2AM decisions may look a little less classy.

Here is a list of decisions that are better at 2AM than in the light of the next day:

- Ordering a pizza with every topping on the menu and then eating it
- Texting your high school boyfriend/ girlfriend and then their new boyfriend/girlfriend
- Putting your head through a wall

- Taking your pants off at a party because you vomited on the pants you wore out
- Prank calling your professor without blocking your number
- Accidently sending your grandma a picture of your girlfriend's boobs
- Stealing a cop car
- Finally deciding to set fire to your friend's sweater that you hate
- Calling your old babysitter just to check in
- Writing and submitting a paper that someone told you was due two hours and one minute earlier
- Breaking into the biology lab
- Falling asleep on the couch in the common area of your dorm...naked

The vast majority of this book is based on things that seem like a great idea, especially late at night. But topping the list of things you should maybe think twice about, and by *topping the list* I mean *somewhere on the list in no particular order*, is hooking up with your roommate's ex.

Your roommate's ex is the human-equivalent of the forbidden fruit. You can't be with your roommate's ex without potentially causing some serious damage to the relationship you have with your roommate. But we want what we can't have. The grass is always greener on the other side. One man's trash is another man's treasure. *Something something something*. All of those sayings originated from the first time someone hooked up with their roommate's ex (no they didn't). And all that **forbidden-ness** just makes that person way sexier. Especially at 2AM.

Look, if you and roommate's ex can't control your **chimpanzee-lust** then at least be smart and discreet about what you're doing. Make sure the lights go out in that basement party you're at before you slobber all over those off-limits lips. Don't discuss your escapades with other people. Leave before the roommate wakes up. And, for God's sake, don't hook up in the same room as the roommate.

So, have your secrets, but don't be a **real d-bag** and flaunt it in anyone's face while also considering the likelihood that roommate and ex may just get back together. Also remember, people talk even when they swear they won't. So weigh and measure the pros and cons of this encounter before taking the plunge and then maybe take a cold shower OR go hook up with someone else.

BTW, if you decide to break-up with your boyfriend for one night and have sex with his fraternity brother nicknamed Stinky Pete on that breakup night and, *oops, get herpes* from Stinky Pete and then get back together with your boyfriend the next day, things will probably get awkward... for everyone.

110:

Don't Get Fat

You know what's not healthy? **Pizza smoth-ered in ranch dressing**. When you get to college your culinary appetites will change. You may find that those pressed "chicken" sandwiches at the dining hall are masterpieces and that on chicken sandwich day you should eat in bulk because it won't be chicken sand-wich day again until the following Thursday. You might be willing to commit a *minor felony* for a steak and cheese. You might think that just because it says *mango* on your smoothie cup that you're actually consuming fresh tree ripened tropical fruit rather than mango flavored ice cream. You might think that french fries smothered in liq-uid "cheese" is a good midnight snack choice. But let me assure you, **garbage eater**, none of these things are true or a good idea, and also, if your liquid cheese is still liquid when you wake up the next day with some in your hair, on your sheets, and decorating the wall then it isn't actu-ally cheese.

It's hard to eat healthy in college. I mean there are things like **pot and beer** that make eating healthy almost as hard as showing up for an 8:30AM class. There are other things too, like the opportunity to make your own decisions about what you should eat or the simultaneously great and awful fragrance that wafts out of the dining hall air vents as you walk by—somehow always smelling like greasy hamburgers regardless of what's on the menu. It's super hard to make a healthy choice when the dining hall offers eighty-six miles of unhealthy options and one small counter of healthy things with four **super annoying and energetic people** waiting in line for their grilled chicken, brown rice, and steamed broccoli. I mean that's basically setting you up for failure.

Look, once in a while these things might be exactly what you need, and *good for you*, go for it, you have to have a balance in your life. But just because there's three-day-old shredded lettuce on top of your taco pizza **doesn't make it a salad**, especially after you smash up a bag of Doritos to cover the browning lettuce. Remember that vegetables are not the enemy, have something healthy to go along with that bag of Twizzlers that you just dipped in peanut butter and for the love of God, drink some water!

111:

Don't Be So
Freakin' Lazy

You will *never* have more free time in your life than when you are in college. After one week it will probably be hard to even remember how you managed to get to high school by 7:30 in the morning, go to class until 2:30- 3:00 then play sports or do clubs or go to work for a couple of hours, followed by homework before finally getting everything done at 11 pm. Somehow that **nightmare** gets locked in a small corner of your brain once you realize that you only have to go to class from 11:45—1:00 on Mondays and Wednesdays and have the balls to complain that Tuesdays and Thursdays are your *long* days when you have class from 2:00-4:00…**WAH WAH.** So what the hell do you do with the other 22+ hours of the day? Eh, nothing really.

The naps you were so offended by as a kid suddenly become a necessary part of your day. The action, or inaction, of playing Call of Duty for seven straight hours seems like a good time-filler. Laying on your bed listening to music is a 1970's idea that makes total sense now. Binge watching Netflix feels mandatory so that you keep up with what's current even though you're watching 90's sitcoms. But here's an alternative idea, **lazy ass**, go to the gym!

Colleges have these beautiful, state-of-the-art fitness facilities. You remember, you saw it on your campus tour when you vowed to develop a serious work-out regimen and come back home for your first break freshman year looking like Hercules or Aphrodite. So utilize them, go work-out. You know what's outside? Fresh air! Go breathe it in, bring your Frisbee, you know you've been wanting to bust that thing out of the package since you bought it in August while imagining yourself glistening in the sun, making outstanding highlight-reel-level catches and throws in front of group of impressed onlookers. Do something active—there's plenty of time for your Xbox when you're home for winter break, bored as hell, wishing you were back at school!

Here are some other ideas for what you can do besides laying in your bed watching YouTube:

- Do your laundry
- Visit a friend in the dorm that your crush lives in
- Make your bed, jk lol
- Play hacky-sack since college is the only acceptable time in life to actually play hacky-sack

- Play the guitar or hang out near someone who is and pretend you're friends with them because they're way cooler than you
- Wash the dishes you left in the sink two days ago
- Go to extra help
- Get an STD test
- Visit a professor during their office hours just to say hello, they'll remember the visits when it's time to submit their grades
- Go to a sporting event (you don't even have to be sober you just have to be vertical)
- Or how about this... do your homework, stooge, you still have to actually pass your classes!!

Being lazy at college is **super easy**; college life is just so conducive to laying around. But everyone once in a while try to get your heart pumping and force the sludge in your veins to move around a little bit. You'll feel better about every part of your life if you do and, perhaps more importantly, people will be very impressed by you and, of course, other people's opinions of you are super important **(jk).**

112:

Don't Get Arrested

Here's an idea: **don't get arrested in college**. Now you may be thinking that you are above that, there's no way you're gonna get arrested, you're perfect, you're too privileged for that. Newsflash, **you're not**. Another newsflash, cops near college campuses know what you're doing because they've been seeing it for years. This might be your first time at your school but it isn't theirs.

You know those **huge parties** on beautiful sunny days where everyone is buff and in bathing suits, squirting hoses, laughing, playing loud music, and jumping into baby pools filled with Jell-O? Yeah well the cops know about them too, they know when they're gonna happen and they have their supply of **rubber gloves and vomit bags** all stacked up in their cruisers just waiting for it to get crazy. You know those nights when you're feeling extra rowdy and think doing shots of peppermint schnapps and smashing mailboxes seems like the greatest and most original plan ever? Yeah well the cops know about those too and their eyes are already rolling in preparation to hear the excuses you make for *not* doing something that they actually see you doing. You know how clothing becomes **optional** when you're wasted? Well the cops don't think it is.

If you're wondering how to avoid getting arrested in college, try these few tips:

- If you're partying in the yard behind some off campuses houses and the cops roll up, drop your cup and slowly walk away
- Don't shout unintelligible profanity at a local just mowing his lawn
- If you've taken your clothes off and start to walk outside, stop, and go back inside
- Don't urinate on the doorstep of a local police station
- Don't challenge people to an old school street fight when they are just coming out of church
- If you sound like you're having a stroke when you talk, stay indoors
- Don't try to steal a cop's gun cuz you think it will be hilarious
- Don't offer to take a Breathalyzer because you're drunk enough to think you can outsmart it

🥤 Don't give the finger to everyone you see

🥤 Don't do any of the things discussed in this book

Listen, **hot shot**, the cops are way ahead of you so respect them, don't walk the streets with your red solo cups, and stay the hell out of jail because no one wants to be doing community service while everyone else is belly flopping down a vodka-laden slip-n-slide.

113:

Don't Go Ice-Skating When You're Drunk

Alcohol makes a lot of things seem like a good idea. Like creeping through a cemetery at night and then trying to climb over a barbed-wire fence when you think the cops are coming, fooling around with someone in a building under construction only to get itchy insulation stuck on your bare ass, dressing up like Batman for Halloween night then going back to someone else's dorm and having to walk home the next morning in your Batman costume. I get it; I've been there. But ice-skating while drunk is definitely *not* a good idea. You know what happens when you ISUI (Ice Skate Under the Influence)? You tear your rotator cuff.

Hey man, we've all watched ice-skating in the Olympics. We've seen hockey on TV. Those people make it look pretty darn easy so, naturally, a bunch of beers only confirm that prancing across frozen water with knives on your feet seems like a piece of cake. Well it isn't. It's an unnatural activity only fit for people who came out of the womb with ice skates on, *like Canadians.*

If you try to ice skate sober then you have a fighting chance of surviving the activity in good, or at least decent, physical health. You're in the right frame of mind and know to grab onto the railing, you can brace yourself when you fall, you can accept the reasons for wearing a helmet. But when you ice-skate drunk, helmets are for losers, railings are for babies, and bracing yourself when you fall is a physical impossibility. Trust me, if you ice-skate drunk you're gonna end up with some kind of medical contraption strapped to some part of your body...*unless you're Canadian.*

BTW, I'm not concerned about those of you that **get high and go ice-skating** because let's face it, you're just gonna be sitting on the second bleacher eating a giant hot pretzel and drinking a gallon and a half of orange soda while watching drunk ice-skaters blow out their knees, all while wondering how you got there.

114:

Don't Plan On Being A Virgin Forever

Oh boy, *virginity*. That's still a thing huh? Okay college virgins, this one is for the **three of you**. I think it's reasonable to imagine that when you are born your parents may have had an expectation that you would stay a virgin forever. I think that even when you get older and they start fantasizing about grandchildren that they secretly believe you will provide them with grandchildren while still maintaining your virginity, ya'know in like some **Jesusy-type-of-way**. It's possible that they instilled a belief in you that you should wait until marriage to have sex, or preferably, never have sex but also give them grandchildren. This kind of thing happens with parents. It's kind of a knee jerk reaction because they really don't want to imagine you rubbing bodies with someone else while **making monkey noises.** Okay, I get it, it's a horrible thing for parents to think about, but that doesn't mean that you shouldn't think about it.

I am absolutely not here to encourage a college virgin to just **rip off their chastity belts** as soon as their parents drive off campus that first day. Rather, I am suggesting to, perhaps, manage your expectations. If you go to college with this hard and fast rule that you will also leave college *intact*, that's great, I hope you can do it. Well not *do it*, but be successful in keeping your virginity.

So in order to help you on your quest, here is a list of things to be aware of that can make the average 18-22 year-old-body crave sex:

- The wind is blowing
- Alcohol consumption
- Hearing your friends wild stories
- It's Tuesday
- No parents are around to stop you
- You're awake
- You love the way you look in an outfit
- You're asleep
- You're surrounded by people you're attracted to....constantly
- It's morning
- You just brushed your teeth
- You got a good grade on a test
- You failed a test
- It's afternoon

🥃 Your room is clean
🥃 You had a salad for lunch
🥃 It's nighttime
🥃 You have a pulse

In college, if you're a virgin it may seem like you're the only one. You may feel like a sexual Sasquatch, an eighth wonder of the world, something the government is holding captive in Area 51, and **maybe you are.** But you're probably *not* the *only* virgin. And if you're ready to lose your virginity when you get to college, go for it my friend, but maybe manage your expectations for your first time because it's probably gonna be really quick and not totally blow your mind so maybe lower the bar a little bit.

It's extremely normal to physically want to have sex. It's also normal to mentally and emotionally want to have sex. So if you want to have sex with someone who also wants to have sex with you, then **steal a condom** and have sex. But if you are mentally and emotionally, maybe even spiritually, *not* ready to have sex then don't. If your body is saying *yes* but your belief system is saying *no* then think it through, think about which part of yourself to listen to, think about how you might feel afterward. If any part of that thinking is negative then just take a cold shower, maybe eat four burritos, and wait until the thinking is all positive. And hey man, just do you (pun intended).

115:

Don't Drunk-Dial Your Parents

Parents love it when you call them from college. It makes them feel special. They love hearing your voice; it comforts them and lets them know you're doing okay. I encourage phone calls home for the good it does for all the people involved but please, **for the love of God**, do *not* drunk-dial your parents.

The thing about alcohol is that it can put you **in the mood** to share your love in a lot of ways. Like sharing your love of strangers by making out with a few of them or sharing your love of exotic foods eating a S'mores Pop Tart smothered in Cheez Whiz or sharing your love of fast movement by skateboarding down a hill that ends at a busy intersection when you've *never* actually skate-boarded before. There are a lot of ways you may choose to share your love and at some point in your college career you may think that you should share your love of your parents by calling them up after you drank thirty beers and declaring that love to them.

Here's the thing about parents, **they aren't as dumb as you think they are.** They probably know when the phone rings at midnight that you aren't coming home from a late night in the library and just feel like catching up. They know when you're slurring your speech that you're probably not currently having a **stroke.** They know that this sudden outpouring of affection and gratitude for their amazing parenting skills is likely a revelation you discovered at the bottom of the **five dollar bottle of vodka** you just mixed with an open can of Pepsi you found on your windowsill.

Drunk-dialing your parents will result in one of two things. Either your parents will laugh at what an **idiot** you are or they'll be pissed, drive up to school, and pack your shit up to send you to **rehab.** And, I should point out, that when you drunk-dial your parents, you are exponentially more likely to share a story with them that you will probably regret sharing later. So save the phone calls for Sunday afternoons or walking home from class or some moment of sobriety. Trust me they'll think you're the greatest, which is way better than them thinking **you're a drunk asshole.**

116:

Don't Think Your Professors Haven't Heard That St. Patrick's Day Excuse Before

St. Patrick's Day is not a national holiday. It's not a religious holiday. It's not a day off. The banks aren't closed. The market is still trading. And most of you are not all that Irish. But somewhere along the line, St. Patrick's Day has become a widely recognized day of **drunken foolishness** for college students. This day of foolishness will mostly fall somewhere between Monday and Friday while you are in college, it always seems to work out that way, which means that you will probably have class. So now you are faced with the lifelong dilemma that all college students face, do you go to class on St. Patrick's Day or do you start *drinking green beer* at 8am?

Friends, this is not a new dilemma and your college professors are acutely aware of it because they literally make a living out of being smart and thus have March 17th circled in red on their calendars long before you do. March 17th is St. Patrick's Day, **genius,** just in case you couldn't figure that out.

You might have an assignment due specifically on that day. Your professor might decide to award the conscientious students who make it to class with the answer to a question they'll put on the final. They might throw out some extra credit points, which will come in handy in another month. But most of all, they know who's there and who isn't and they know that if you aren't there that you're sitting on someone's porch in a ridiculous and possibly offensive St. Patrick's Day t-shirt making **bad decisions.**

If you decide to skip class, don't insult your professor with some nonsense excuse the next time you see them, or in a preemptive email the day before, or worse yet a drunk email the day of. It's better just to suffer the consequences and move on. But if you're dumb enough to try to create an excuse, let me assure you, your professor has heard them all before.

Here's a list of common "Sorry I Missed Class" excuses:

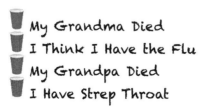

My Grandma Died
I Think I Have the Flu
My Grandpa Died
I Have Strep Throat

My Roommate's Grandma Died
My Alarm Didn't Go Off
My Roommate's Grandpa Died
My Car Wouldn't Start
My Dog Died
I Couldn't Find My Keys
My Roommate's Dog Died
Someone Told Me Class Was Cancelled
My Grandma's Dog Died
My Roommate Got Food Poisoning
My Dog's Grandma Died
I Lost My Shoes
Someone's Grandma Died
I Might Have Polio

I should point out that if you think you're gonna have the best of both worlds by partying and then going to class, you should probably rethink that one. If you have sticky dried on green Jell-O shot smeared across the side of your cheek, your professor is going to notice. They'll smell it if you stink like a brewery. They'll know that water bottle you've been making out with for the last twenty minutes does not contain water. So maybe just wait until after class to party. But if you do decide to cut then own it, excuses are for freshmen and people who haven't read this book.

117:

Don't Show Your
Fake ID To The Cops

I'm super happy that you are smart enough to go to college, good for you, **you're winning in the game of life.** But if you're dumb enough to show your fake ID to the cops when they stop you on the street for walking like you're a **one-legged pirate** staggering through wet cement, then you deserve the repercussions.

Fake IDs are only good for two things—buying alcohol and getting into a bar. They are not intended to be used in real life situations like applying for a Work Visa in Italy or buying a boat or whatever dumb thing you can think of. And they are *definitely not* intended to actually present to the cops. Fake IDs are not legal, that's why the Department of Motor Vehicles only gives you a real ID with your real birthdate, name and face. And if you show something **not legal** to the cops they will laugh in your face and then arrest you. When you're in college, and also any other part of your life, you should make an effort to avoid being arrested.

One of the classic ways **dumbo college students** get arrested is by showing their fake ID to the cops. Bro, I don't care how good you think your fake is, the cops know that you are either: **A.** not 45 years old, **B.** not the ethnicity listed on your fake, **C.** not from France, or **D.** definitely not named *Delores*, no one's is. They also know that your Staten Island accent doesn't seem to match up with your South Carolina license.

On the list of legal things, I'm pretty sure fake IDs are not included. So don't be so dumb, when a cop asks you for your ID show them the real one, trust me, you'll get in a lot less trouble if you do, Delores Sucknuts, M.D.

118:
Don't Set Furniture On Fire

It should be **pretty obvious** that you shouldn't take a match to your coffee table, however *setting furniture on fire* is something that I've come across....more than once. There's something about college that brings out the pyromaniac in people. Look, it's so awesome that your school's hockey team won the National Championship for the first time in history. This is a great thing and I'm so proud of you for being such a dedicated hockey fan for that *one game* that you feel the need to celebrate your school's victory by throwing your couch out into the street, dousing it with lighter fluid and setting it ablaze. But take my advice and leave the torches to the toothless townspeople in Beauty and the Beast and just punch out the ceiling tiles like a normal person.

If you happen to sit on a futon that you vowed never to sit on because your friend urinated on it two weeks ago, please do not ban together with your support group, carry that futon down to the river and set it on fire. And then, for the love of God, when that futon starts drifting toward the river bank and its dried up overhanging trees please do not run away screaming as if not being there will ensure that the dead shit on the side of the river won't catch fire.

Here's a list of things you shouldn't set on fire in college:

- Your dorm
- Your hair
- The hair of anyone in your vicinity
- Your thumbnail, just kidding it's unavoidable when lighting a bowl
- Your textbooks
- Your professor
- Your bedding
- Your desk
- Your roommate
- A pool table
- Poop
- Or any other thing that exists in the world

There are a lot of things that you *should* do in college, but **setting shit on fire** is definitely not one of them. So chill out, **Smokey the Bear**. Go tie your shirt around your head and run wild, it's a lot safer than breaking up a small table thinking it'll just make a small fire until you realize that small table has been painted with some nuclear chemical producing flames that can be seen in space. **Dumbass.**

119:

Don't Expect Your Security Deposit Back

I love the **optimism** of a college student. Your positive attitude and total naivety are super endearing. When you send in that security deposit for your dorm or your off-campus house, you're probably thinking, *Sweet, I'll totally get that $750 back just in time for summer!* Well, **optimist,** I hate to break it to you but that money was spent before you finished your second week in September.

All that toilet clogging, all that dried on pudding that took the paint off the walls because you didn't feel like wiping it off when you flung it there, all of that aggressive falling into the shower curtains, all of that punching out the window screens to try to force an illegal air conditioner in your window, cost you your security deposit. Sure, you might think that because you replaced the closet door that you **drunkenly** wrenched off the hinges that your landlord wouldn't notice the hole your head created in the wall behind it. You could think that the smoke detector you disabled because it was **interfering with your bong hits** would go overlooked. Maybe you'd even consider that people would think the lyrics of *your* favorite song written in permanent marker on your cinderblock wall were there when you moved in. But, alas, none of those things are going unnoticed in your room or your friend's room, or the room of that kid you never really liked, and they are all being fixed with your security deposits.

If you think logically about drinking, it's really just like throwing money away because you drink and then pee or vomit it out. Pretty much the same thing with food, you eat it and then *poop* it's gone, though consuming food does actually allow you to live, but I digress. **So security deposits are pretty much the urine and fecal matter of your college tuition.** It's all getting flushed right down the toilet never to be seen again. So plan on working all summer long because you won't be living off of this year's security deposit and you're gonna have to pay for next years.

120:

Don't Apply Make-up
After Your Start Drinking

Listen up. If you are planning to drink alcohol *and* you are planning to wear make-up and do your hair for the drinking event, please do yourself a favor and get all dolled-up *before* you start drinking. FYI, if you roll into the dining hall at 9:30AM with a bold red lip, full cat eyes, and an up-do, people are gonna know pretty quickly that you started drinking before breakfast.

Here's the thing—you're all probably pretty great-looking already. After all, you have youth and excitement and hope and dreams on your side, all of these things make you look awesome. If you feel the need to add some eyeliner or fill in your brows, I get it; do what makes you feel good. If you feel like curling your hair and giving it some extra volume, do it. But please do all of these things *before* you commence the consumption of booze. I mean, unless you are going for the **drag-queen look.**

For some strange reason, alcohol makes you think that you'd look better with a maroon lip outline and pink lip-gloss. It makes you sad that you've never touched the blue eye shadow in your pallet of 58 colors and, therefore, decide to remedy that sadness by caking on most of the entire little square of it. Alcohol reminds you that you could use a *little* color on your cheeks that haven't seen the sun in three and a half months, but it makes you forget exactly what *little* means. If you're feeling brave, and since you've been drinking I'd imagine you are, you might decide, after three gin and tonics, that today is the day you'll try contouring or the smoky-eye look. Friends, trust me, **none of this is a good idea.**

When you see yourself on Insta the next day, you'll know what I'm talking about. So put down the blush brush when you pick up the pinot, you already look **gorgeous!** And also, stay away from adding the airbrush app to your glamour shots because you'll end up looking like any character in an anime movie.

BTW, if you're planning to **get high** and apply make-up, I'm not worried about you because let's be real, you know as well as I do that you're never gonna end up putting on that make-up. You'll be sitting on the corner of your bed, eating a bag of Cheetos, drinking a jug of milk and vaping, all while fixating on your drunken roommate as she literally paints a replica of the solar system on her face.

121:

Don't Think You're Not Gonna Dress Up For Halloween

You probably stopped thinking that dressing up for Halloween was cool in fifth grade. That's normal and you're right, that *is* the last time that dressing up for Halloween was cool or **socially acceptable.** Right around the time when you thought you'd throw on a Jason mask with your regular clothes just to pillage for candy and spray Silly String all over the neighborhood is right around the time when you became **too douchy** for your neighbors to answer the door when you came begging for sweets. But then college comes around and suddenly Halloween becomes a national holiday. For the record, in college, Halloween ranks just behind the *national holiday* of St. Patrick's Day and right in front of *any day of the week.*

Halloween in college is big. REALLY BIG. Sometimes a four-day event. And that doesn't mean four days of the same costume, because let's face it, there's probably someone's vomit on at least two days of those costumes. Nah, Halloween is a multi-day, **multi-costume extravaganza.** Are you going to be trick-or-treating? No, don't be ridiculous, but there will be treats and some of you will probably look like you're ready to turn tricks. Halloween in college is fun, you get to look crazy or sexy or funny or clever and basically anything in your closet or room can be combined into some kind of costume. So be prepared to dress up—it's the only other time after fifth grade that it's cool to do so.

When choosing your costume(s), here are some things to consider:

▼ Maybe shy away from the cat ears paired with a bra and hot pants. That isn't as classy as you think on IG.

▼ Maybe shy away from a toga with nothing underneath. That isn't as sexy as you think when you fall over, spread eagle into a thorn bush.

▼ Maybe shy away from masks. They are sexy and mysterious but when you take them off to make out with the person who has no idea who you are, your face is gonna be red and sweaty and will probably smell like plastic and lacrosse cleats. Also a mask is only not annoying for three minutes.

Maybe shy away from anything big and bulky. The parties you're going to go to are gonna be crowded; don't be the asshole dressed like a fat banana taking up half the room.

I want you to have fun on your extended Halloween binge but don't forget the most important thing… if you don't go home to your house or dorm or apartment at the end of the night then you will have to go back to your house or dorm or apartment in the bright, unforgiving sunshine of the next day…still wearing last night's costume and not looking cute at all. Gobs of skeleton make up are only good for the two hours immediately following the application; the next morning you'll look like a blob of molding clay. So go do your thing but think through the unplanned end of the night sexcapades, and for God's sake, don't get arrested because there is no way that a drunken, adult-sized Power Ranger slumped in a jail cell is a good look.

122:

Don't Adopt The Accent Of The Area You Go To College In

This is almost too annoying to talk about but if you go to school in Rochester and come back home to Long Island with a crazy Western New York accent, everyone has permission to **slap you in the face.** You have the obligation to be slapped in the face if you're whooping it up all year at Georgia Tech and go back to Ohio in May talkin' all Southern-like. If you spend your college years in Maryland and think you can go back to Texas with the weird, indescribable Maryland accent, it may become a law that you get slapped in the face. Stop it.

You're **not from** the places you go to school in (unless you are then this post doesn't apply to you) so stop it with that ludicrous accent. Go back to your roots, be yourself. I'm not saying it's a bad thing to tone down your Staten Island accent when you've had some exposure to the world, but fully adopting a Florida one is absolutely not gonna work. You know what you'll end up sounding like? **An asshole.**

I should say that it can be expected that when you're drunk your college accent might come out at home, just like your home accent might come out at college, that's to be expected but within three months after graduation you better plan to be cured of that affliction. **Get your shit together** and stop talking like you're from the Black Hills of South Dakota, nobody is! Honestly, is anyone actually *from* the Black Hills of South Dakota? **Talk normally!**

123:

Don't Think You're Not Gonna See Someone Again

Oh boy, we've all learned this lesson *one too many times*. So here's the deal—the world is a lot smaller than you think and your campus, even if it seems big, is barely a dot on a map. This revelation often comes to light one day after you hook up with someone in a way that you are not super proud of. You may have hooked up with someone that you don't actually like when you're sober, someone you don't know, did something a little crazier than you would've done ordinarily, the list goes on and on but you get the picture. And even though last night you hooked up with someone you have never seen before you can almost guarantee that they'll be sitting on a porch with their friends day drinking when you randomly walk by alone, looking and feeling **rough** from the night before.

Guess who's gonna be at the party you go to the next night? Yup, your special friend from the night before. You know who's gonna walk past you in the dining hall the exact moment you splash spaghetti sauce all over your face? You guessed it, *Mr. The Other Night*. This happens all the time, I mean ALL THE TIME, too much, so be prepared to roll your eyes and laugh it off.

Here's a list of things you shouldn't do when you unexpectedly see your random hookup:

- Jump behind a bush that's smaller than your body
- Choke on your gum
- Make a pterodactyl noise
- Shoot beer out of your nose
- Turn your back to them even though everyone around you has their front to them
- Fall down
- Walk into a wall
- Run away
- Pretend you've never seen them (or their private parts) before

And also don't do the opposite of all these things like:

- Run in slow motion toward them like you're in a movie
- Propose marriage
- Jump in front of them

🥤 Tackle them
🥤 Ask to meet their parents
🥤 Scream their name to get their atten-
   tion because you probably don't
   know their real name
🥤 Hump them

Listen, when you inevitably see this person again, just be cool. Say hello, give a nod of acknowledgment and maybe a little wink if you're cool enough to pull it off. BTW, this post isn't just about the people you hook up with in college even though they may be **interviewing you for a job in six years.** It's also about everyone you come in contact with. You will see people again, you will meet people who know people you went to school with and both of these things happen for the rest of your life. So, here's the lesson…don't be a dick. Go have fun, be wild, be hilarious but be nice too. Fifteen years after graduation you want people to say, "Yeah I knew her in college, she was really funny", you don't want them to say "Yeah I knew him in college, hopefully he's bald because he was a huge tool."

124:

Don't Get High And
Go To The Library

Look, if you want to spend your college days **smok-ing pot** that's your thing, I'm not gonna judge you for it. I won't judge you for anything that you do in college, unless you're hurting someone else then **I'll judge the shit out of you**, but if you're doing you and not harming someone then do you, go for it. But if you do spend your days and nights as the mayor of La La Land then maybe keep it to yourself and the citizens of your hazy dreamland. Maybe don't, for example, **get high and go to the library** on campus.

Okay, at first glance this may seem like a great activity. At first glance it may seem like getting high and going to the library will lead to a story you can write about as a cautionary tale years later in a book about **what not to do in college**. At first glance you may think you can participate in this activity without impacting any of the people in the library who are doing what they should be doing at college, aka studying. But trust me, when you bust through those classy big oak doors and fall into a raucous fit of laughter while swigging huge bottles of water to quell your cotton mouth, people are gonna see you and they're gonna know what's up. **Literally.**

Remember, the only people in the library cracking up while blindly flipping through the book of Japanese art they just grabbed off the shelf to look inconspicuous, bumping into the stacks, and trying desperately not to look high, are the people who are high.

Believe it or not, on the list of great ideas, this one doesn't actually rank that high. Here's why:

- You know who's often at the library? Students who will be super judgey of your recreational choices because they're not blowing their parents $200K out the window through paper towel rolls filled with dryer sheets.

- You know who's often at the library? Professors. One of which is the guy who lead the class you skipped that afternoon to get high.

- You know who's often at the library? Religious people. The ones walking around in the priest ensembles when it isn't Halloween who either teach or provide guidance for the people who aren't currently high like your dumb ass.

▌ You know who's often at the library? That hot guy that you want to trick into thinking you're super studious just because he's super studious and also not high.

▌ You know who's often at the library? The T.A. of your physics class that you're almost failing and only took because the T. A. is record-setting hot and you have a teacher–student fantasy (who doesn't?) that you're pretty sure you can lock down with Hot T.A.

There are people in the library and not one of them is high. So when you decide to go sit on the soccer field one night with the assistant mayor and chief of police of La La Land to get high, go to the dining hall afterward like the rest of the stoners and leave the library to the nerds who are going to rule the world one day.

125:

Don't Create A List Of People You And Your Friends Have Hooked Up With

So it's pretty common knowledge that when people hook up there's a good possibility that the parties involved in said hook up will likely tell one or two or twenty-five people about it. This is usually the case with one-nighters. Not so much with relationships because it's kind of weird to tell people about how you hooked up with your boyfriend or girlfriend—nobody cares about that and stop rubbing it in people's faces that you're getting it on the regular while other people are in a month-long drought. But one-nighters are salacious. They're crazy or unexpected and you feel the need to share, to maybe brag a little bit or get some reassurance that your hook up partner isn't totally awful during the sober moments in life, even though they probably are. But here's a word of caution: be mindful of what you say and how you disseminate the information.

Please trust me on this one. TRUST ME. If you and your friends want to lay around your dorm room regaling each other with stories of your sexual prowess, great, have fun. But keep your **mildly exaggerated** tales as just stories you *talk* about. Do not at any point make a list of the vast numbers of people you all have hooked up with and DEFINITELY do not create a ranking system that is defined on that list and used to categorize all the people who were blessed enough to partake in the awesomeness that your bodies have provided. You know what will happen to that list? One Sunday morning you will go to take it out to add your weekend's conquests and that list won't be there. You know where it will be? It'll be floating like the photocopied pages of the Burn Book all around campus as the object of lots and lots and lots of conversation.

Some people will see their name on that list and be upset by their ranking, which can't possibly end well. Some people will see their name on that list and be super stoked about their ranking and then not make much of an effort for their next hookup because they just assume they're awesome without even trying, which can't possibly end well for their new partner. Some people will see their boyfriend's or girlfriend's name on that list...**oops.** This list is only going to because problems, believe me, **ain't nothing good coming out of this list.** So pass your stories down as oral history/ modern day urban legends, but do not write them on paper or in a document on your computer or create a private Facebook page about it or put it in a group text, because one day, way too many people are gonna see that list. And BTW, don't be afraid to *not* kiss and tell? But also, **good for you and your friends** for being sexy enough to even think about a list!

126:

Don't Think Parent's Weekend Isn't Gonna Be Awesome

You think your parents are **lame?** I don't blame you, a lot of young people think their parents are lame. But I can guarantee that your parents probably don't think they're lame and they definitely didn't think they were lame when they were your age. If you're in college now or will be soon, there's a decent possibility that your parents also went to college. And if your parents went to college, guess what? They probably did everything that you're doing. Full disclosure, I may be projecting on that one.

Here's the point—if you think Parent's Weekend is going to be all campus tours and campus cookouts and church you are probably not entirely correct. Sure, most parents will stick to that plan, but there will be a handful of parents reliving their glory days and trying to prove that they still got it. And *those* parents are fun as shit.

When you go to college, everything changes, including your relationship with your parents. You're older, you're more mature (or trying to convince people you are), you've had more experiences, you're more worldly, you've expanded your horizons, you can—*occasionally*—take care of yourself and your parents get that and they're excited about it. Parents also know that college isn't necessarily an example of the real world; they know it's a blip in time and something about that makes parents let their hair down and only good things can come from that.

If it's Parent's Weekend and your parents want to go out to a bar with you and your friends, your answer should be a resounding YES! First of all, **they buy the drinks** and your poor ass could use a benefactor for the night. Second of all, your friends will think that your parents are the coolest because their parents are at the Holiday Inn resting up for breakfast with the President the next morning. Third of all, **they buy the drinks.** And fourth of all, **they buy the drinks.**

So invite your parents up for Parent's Weekend and get excited about it. Let them run wild and relive their college days or experience college life for the first time as they imagined it would have been. And remember, parents are people too and after a few drinks at the local bar, your parents will probably let some stories slip that you can use on them in the future when you're home and **stumbling in at 3am**! Oh and BTW, if you go out the night before Parent's Weekend and you wake up on the day your parents are due to arrive with a huge scrape up the middle of your face that neither you nor your friends know how you got, just tell your parents that you tripped while out for a jog, let them think you sometimes do healthy things... **what they don't know can't hurt them!**

127:

Don't Stare At The Sun

This isn't some deep philosophical statement about your future or trying to be a celebrity or whatever the smart of the meaning "*Don't Stare At The Sun*" is. I mean this literally. Literally don't stare at the sun. You may ask yourself how this one ended up on this list of remarkably well-developed, totally useful life lessons. Well it's simple. It seems like **every year** there is an eclipse that only happens once every **525,000** years. I don't know if anyone else has noticed this but seriously, there has to be a yearly once-in-a-lifetime eclipse, either that or I've lived a shitload of lifetimes and didn't realize it, ya'know because I peed too many of my brain cells down the toilet in college.

So here's what's gonna happen. This miraculous event will occur some warm late August day during your first week back at school when you've been making up for three and a half months of non-freedom by drinking beer for breakfast…and lunch…and dinner followed by two slices of taco pizza. It's two days before classes start, you've only slept for the hours between 8 and 10 in the morning for the last week with maybe a 3-5PM nap sprinkled in and you have long since forgotten everything you learned in your mandatory science course from the semester before. Then you combine your lifestyle with the fact that you definitely know better than every specialist on the news leading up to the big day telling you that if you stare at the sun you will go blind. Psh, what do they know? **Meteorology isn't real.**

So the eclipse comes and what happens? Do you take the time to fashion an eclipse-viewing device out of a cereal box? **Nah,** too lazy. Do you buy eclipse viewing glasses? **Nah,** too expensive. Do you skip the eclipse all together because you know for a fact this happens every year and you'll just catch the next one? Maybe. But if you don't fall into that last group then you'll probably just nut up, grab Mother Nature by the **boob** and stare boldly at that 8-gazillion-watt light bulb in the sky waiting, waiting, still waiting for the moment when the world goes dark during the most amazingly rare eclipse ever.

Well, I hate to disappoint, but the world never really goes as dark as we think it's going to. Unless of course you stare at the sun—then it will go dark forever because, **dumb ass,** you'll be blind. Do you know how thick a cornea is? No seriously, do you know because I have no idea. But if I were going to guess I'd say pretty freakin' not thick. If the rays from the sun can penetrate all seven layers of your skin, find some cells, mutate them then brainwash them into forming a cult that not-so-uniquely goes by the name Melanoma, then pump that cult up so much that it bursts to the surface of your skin waving it's middle finger to the world with a **big F-you,** imagine what it can do to your paper-thin cornea. Paper-thin is probably generous but I can't think of anything thinner than paper right now. I'm no scientist because I also forgot everything that I learned in my mandatory science course in college, which was nothing since I cheated off of the guy next to me, but I can imagine that sun-staring cornea just melts away and drips out of your eye along with the tears you'll cry for your lost vision.

I know, it's harsh but **for God's sake** when there's an eclipse make your cereal box viewer or better yet, just wait till the next one, **which should be in about a week.**

128:
Don't Steal Road Signs When You're Drunk

Nobody loves a moron more than I do. I may have been or occasionally might still be a moron. Morons are my people. But if you're feeling the urge to be moronic, maybe don't fulfill that urge by stealing a road sign.

Believe it or not, road signs are not just placed around the neighborhood to be canvases for your poor attempt at graffiti—**no shot** you're really that good with a spray can. They aren't intended to be obstacles on your walk home from the bars. They are not an enemy that you need to aggressively tear down in a sudden display of not-so-well-thought-out dominance—also you're not a silver back gorilla so **cool it** with the displays of dominance. Road signs actually serve a purpose.

Some of these purposes include but are not limited to:

 Not driving off a cliff

- Not plowing through a bunch of ducks randomly crossing a heavily-trafficked street like assholes
- Not breaking the sound barrier with your F-15 jet speed
- Not going straight when the road curves to the right
- Not driving into a lake
- Not missing an exit with a McDonald's
- Not hitting a buffalo—BTW the buffalo won't give a shit but your car will be totaled

All of these are some of the many purposes that road signs serve. They protect people and wildlife. They keep the streets safe-*ish* and if you follow the rules on the signs you may just avoid some jail time. So leave the road signs where they are.

I should mention that if you do accidently steal a construction cone with a light that flashes on top of it, make sure you throw a blanket over that light when the fire alarm in your dorm goes off at 3AM because nothing wakes up **300 half-dead college students** standing outside in the quad outside like a flashing yellow beacon coming from your window just begging for the RAs to come in and slap a big fat fine on your ass. Oh, one more thing, if you happen to run across a sign that says "High Street Under Construction" you should probably steal that. Obviously.

129:

Don't Try Changing Things Up By Infiltrating A Local Bar

You know who hates loud, drunk-ass college students? **Locals.** You know, the people who live and work in the town that you use as your toilet bowl after experimenting with Long Island Iced Teas. Please note, Long Island Iced Teas are not actually iced tea, they're just a **bunch of brown liquor** and they have absolutely nothing to do with Long Island. But the locals, sitting hunched at the bar wearing John Deer hats un-ironically while sipping their Pabst Blue Ribbon already know that and they know that thirty minutes after you enter the bar, you're gonna be the absolute worst.

Here's why locals and college kids like you don't mix:

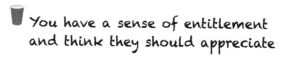 You have a sense of entitlement and think they should appreciate

you for your patronage—they know you have a sense of entitlement and would gladly forgo your summer job money for a little peace after a long day of work.

You dress like dopes in way too tight or way too trendy clothes—they are wearing clothes comfortable enough to let the booze pass through their esophagus.

You think you own the place—they actually own the place.

You think singing Sweet Caroline at the top of your lungs is the greatest part of the night—so do they but you ruined it for them so now they can't sing it because you are.

You will leave the bar and throw up in the street and pee on their lawns—they work in the town and have to clean up your vomit and also you peed on their lawns.

Y'all, I get it. Sometimes going to the same bars with the same people gets stale (no it doesn't, relax). Someone will have this badass idea that you should go to one of the bars that is dedicated to the local population and you think, eh okay. But maybe give them their space to commiserate about how they have brown spots on their lawns from your urine and just about how generally awful you are. I mean since you and the things you **excrete**

from your bodies have taken over their towns like a cancer, the very least you can do is leave them their bars, you have plenty of those.

College students, I love you, your families love you, your friends love you, the college treasurer depositing your tuition checks loves you, **but leave the locals alone.** Go to the bars that are dedicated—by some unwritten rule established way before you got to campus—to the students and let the locals have their peace because let's face it, in a local bar, **you're the worst.**

130:

Don't Think That No One Sees You Making Out In The Bar Just Because *Your* Eyes Are Closed

Ugh. **Gross.** Listen, everybody is sexier after a few drinks and everybody wants to hook up because their libidos are flowing like beer from a freshly tapped keg. But a full on make-out session in a packed bar is just gross. You might think that you and your *partner du jour* are sexy while sampling each other's dental work but nobody else does.

You probably think you're being discreet but let me assure you, the corner of the bar is not a secluded private space. Neither is the middle of the bar. Neither is the side of the pool table in the back of the bar. Neither is the booth that 8 other people are squeezed into. The bathroom stall probably is but you'll be standing in the urine of the 78 people that didn't even try to hit the toilet before you cleverly snuck in there thinking nobody would notice. People notice and also your sneakers now have **Hepatitis C.**

Hey, I'm all for a mutually-agreed-upon bar hookup, but maybe not at the actual bar. A better option would be to flirt at the bar and then go home together. Do what you both want to do in the privacy of a bedroom or at least the semi-privacy of a dorm room—under the covers with the lights out making absolutely no noise. Then one of you will walk home in shame with crazy knots in the back of your hair and "bruises" on your neck like a respectable person.

I should point out that if you are doing the **walk of shame** the next morning, don't really feel the shame. If you both, or all three … or four (no) of you enjoyed yourselves then own it. But don't pretend that no one will notice because the outfit you're wearing is definitely not an 8AM look. And also remember what PDA stands for … Please Don't, Asshole.

131:

Don't Think You're Good At Darts Just Because There's A Dart Board At Your Favorite Bar

Darts at a college bar is probably the **dumbest idea ever.** Actually, darts at any bar is probably the dumbest idea ever. Who thought it would be great to mix alcohol with deadly weapons? Darts are literally the **weapon of choice** for undercover secret agents trying to kill international villains while going completely undetected. They are the ideal toxin-dispensing vehicle that can make a *ten thousand pound bear* fall out of a tree after it lazily wandered into some picturesque town in New Jersey usually near an elementary school. Both of these examples mean that darts should not be present at a college bar.

I am confident in my knowledge of **maybe three things** and one of those things is that you are not good enough at darts to play in a crowded bar after day drinking since 10AM. You aren't some super genius dart shark who's been practicing darts in the basement of your family home since you were nine-months-old. I have a dartboard in my basement and **guess what?** The wall (and floor and ceiling) around the dartboard is full of holes, because there are like four people in the history of the world that are actually good at darts.

Maybe keep these tips in mind:

- If there is anyone within fifty feet of the dartboard, don't play darts.
- If you've had more than one drink, which is probably what you brushed your teeth with before you went out, don't play darts.
- If you're trying to impress someone with your accuracy skills, don't play darts.
- If you're trying to win a bet, don't play darts.
- If you're trying to get out of the bar without a murder conviction, don't play darts.
- If you have to close one eye to see just the actual bullseye, definitely don't play darts.

And please, **for the love of God**, if you own a college bar throw out the damn dartboard. You might be giving these kids cirrhosis but no one gonna notice that for another twenty or thirty years, but a dart hole in the cheek is immediate and it's **nasty.**

132:

Don't Run Naked Anywhere...Ever

Streakers. Since the dawn of time some dumbass has thought running naked in front of a crowd of people was the greatest stunt in the world. Evel Knievel would beg to differ...and so would I. No matter how hard I try I cannot come up with one occasion where running naked in front of other people is a good idea. No wait, that's not true, if you were in the shower and your house exploded into flames then it's okay to run outside naked. But that's the only time. Oh no wait, if you were running through a jungle being chased by a Tyrannosaurus Rex and you had to throw off your clothes so he would chase the scent in a different direction then it's okay. But really that's it. Wait one more thing, if you found six newborn squirrels laying in the snow and you had to use all of your clothes to build them a nest and then run back to your car to get a bag of trail mix that they'll be able to eat next year then that's also acceptable. But **seriously,** those are the only three occasions when it's okay to run around naked in public.

Here's the thing about running naked. **Things bounce around.** And not in a good slow-motion, Baywatch kind of way. They bounce and slap from side to side and up and down in a way that will have people wincing in sympathetic pain at the awkward dance your privates are doing. If you're streaking to try to get a laugh, you'll get one, but it will be one of those laughs where people look out of the side of their eyes silently thinking— This is weird **OR** That's way too small to be shown off like this **OR** What body part is that **OR** Ew **OR** What's this person's end game **OR** Thank God I still have enough battery left on my cell phone to film all of this and post it on social media where it will stay for the rest of his/her life.

See, that last one is the key. Hey listen, back in the gladiator times people could streak across a coliseum to lighten the mood during a lion-gladiator battle to the death, and good for the brave soul who did it. In fairness, half the people in the stands were probably **some degree of naked** anyway so it wasn't such a big deal. But I'm pretty confident that not one of those people had a cell phone to post those flopping body parts on social media. When your grandchildren Google you do you really want them seeing your wiener wiggling around like a tiny eel on a hook? Do you want your elementary school students seeing your boobs bounce up and down but also somehow weirdly side to side? I'm going to imagine that you don't want that.

You know what you also don't want? That girl or guy that you have a crush on seeing you naked for the first time in literally the most unflattering situation. There's no romantic lighting framing your supple body with soft edges. There's no bed to pose on in a way that flatters your abs. There is nothing but the harsh reality that in the blazing midday light, in active motion, **things are not great**. I don't care how perfect you perceive your body to be while standing still in front of a mirror—there ain't no one that looks that great bouncing around. And what if you fall!? Could you imagine the horror if you trip and go sliding front-side-down across the pavement? I started to imagine it but then I forced myself to stop. Also you're probably still wearing your shoes so you're naked from the ankles up like **reverse Amish** and the shoes don't go with your outfit.

And just to drive the point home, it's almost a guarantee that as soon as you round the corner in all your naked glory, a cop will be standing there waiting for you and there's no getting out of that one. So unless you want to end up sitting naked in communal jail cell, dumbass, **for the love of God**, KEEP YOUR CLOTHES ON.

133:

Don't Do Funnels On An Empty Stomach

Do you love to puke? If you do then you can skip this one.

But if you don't think that heaving **beer and bile** out of your mouth so hard that you pop a blood vessel in your eye is the best then you should probably not do funnels on an empty stomach.

Hey man, we've all been there. You **stumble** out of bed in the morning (a.k.a: afternoon), open your bedroom door and there are somehow thirty people in your living room partying like it's 1999, all gathered around that gleaming silver keg and holding a bright red plastic funnel high in the air like it's Simba from the Lion King. Everyone shouts for joy as you make your entrance, one eye still closed, probably only wearing your underwear, a t-shirt and maybe one shoe. You immediately feel excited and welcomed by their joyous reaction to seeing you. They beckon for you to come do a funnel **cuz you're**

soooooo crazy. You rub your other eye open and think—*eh I already missed class so why not*. Well let me tell you why not my friend, because you haven't eaten since that cold slice of pizza you found in the back of the fridge at 2AM which means your stomach is empty and if you do that funnel you will straight up **projectile vomit** on everyone in your living room.

Carbonated beverages were designed to be sipped, maybe even chugged in reasonable quantities. But sipping and chugging all involve swallowing in one to two ounce increments. Carbonated beverages were not designed to be **catapulted by the gallon** through at least six different passageways—maybe two, I don't know anatomy—into your sleepy fist sized stomach with nothing to protect the delicate lining from this vicious...and delicious... assailant.

Similarly, your sleepy fist sized stomach was not designed to receive this blast of carbonated beverage completely without warning. Did you ever walk by a fire hydrant that suddenly burst open flinging you across the street with the force of the water? No of course you haven't, no one has, but it would probably be **hilarious** if it ever did happen. That's what your stomach feels like when you decide to do a funnel without eating first—it feels like getting pummeled by an exploding fire hydrant without any warning (I would imagine). And as soon as that beer hits your stomach your stomach will do what it *was* designed to do and **kick that shit** right out with the same force that it went in.

You won't make it to the bathroom, you won't have time to cover your mouth (which wouldn't do anything anyway except maybe redirect a little beer up your nose), you won't have time to point yourself toward the plastic plant you got as a joke, you will just coat the people around you with regurgitated booze. Gross. Nothing ruins a party like getting thrown up on. Oh who am I kidding, if the party is good even a layer of someone else's vomit won't be a reason to leave. But still…gross.

So do your digestive system and your fellow party-goers a favor and eat some bread before your funnel. Good luck.

134:

Don't Think You're Gonna Have A Wild Threesome In Your Extra Long Twin Dorm Room Bed

Ahhhhh, college. **College is hedonism at its finest.** College was invented in Ancient Greece where orgies and excess were a daily way of life. I mean it totally wasn't, it was invented like 900 years later in some place in Morocco but the Ancient Greece part makes more sense for this scenario because how else can we explain the sexual escapades, booze, togas and sudden profound interest in poetry? So you go to college with this wild idea that your sexual fantasies are going to come true and one of those fantasies is a threesome. Classic.

Here's the thing about threesomes, they seem like a great idea when fantasizing about them. But when that day arrives and the opportunity for a threesome presents itself, things don't exactly go like you imagined.

After the silent shouts of joy screaming in your brain and the theoretical high-fives that your hormones are giving each other, here are some thoughts you will have during your fantasy-come-to-life that you didn't know you'd have:

- Okay, who should I kiss/fondle/etc. first?
- Do I/does he have to change condoms when switching people?
- Goddamn twin sized bed.
- Ow, did I just get elbowed in the face?
- Whose <fill in the blank body part> is this?
- Shit this is a lot of work.
- Are they enjoying this?
- I'm exhausted.
- I shouldn't have eaten that burrito.
- Wait how does this work?
- Are they boxing me out right now?
- What am I supposed to be doing while they're doing that?
- Oh God, I'm cramping.
- I'm so freakin' thirsty.
- Oh shit I'm falling off this baby-sized dorm room bed designed for one person!

Okay, maybe you won't be thinking all of those things but definitely some of them and I'm just making sure you're well prepared. *Sexual experimentation* is something that does happen in college and it's awesome when two or more like-minded people get together to explore their fantasies but if you are one of the many with the *threesome* fantasy, all I'm saying is **manage your expectations**.

You should also know that if you graduate from college without fulfilling this fantasy, you are in the same boat as most other people; this is a tough one to lock down so don't be distressed if it doesn't happen. But if it does happen, remember threesomes are **a lot of work** and require a lot of space so that extra long twin bed you sleep in is not gonna cut it. If there are three of you that want to do this then do it right, talk it out first, know what each other's limitations are, check in with each other while you're checking *in* each other and don't forget to hydrate… just like the Ancient Greeks who founded your college.

Oh, and if you're into rating the people you hook up with by the number system, remember these profound and thoughtful words spoken by someone I know… **"Hey man, if you hook up with a 6 and a 4, that's still a 10."** PREACH.

135:

Don't Take A Class Just Because Your Crush Is Taking It

Wanna know what the hard part about college is? **Class.** I mean just going to class can be hard when it's raining or snowing, or when you're sick or when you don't know where you are when you wake up or when you wake up three hours after class ended. But even those woefully challenging things < *insert eye roll* > are not as hard as the actual class itself. Classes for your major can be hard and those core classes that everyone has to take for some reason (I'm looking at you Western Civ) can be hard too. The **sucky thing** about those classes is that you have to listen during class and do annoying things like study and write papers and learn, all of which thoughtlessly interfere with dollar beer night and we all know that interfering with dollar beer night is some next level bullshit. But, alas, it's college so class and studying and papers and tests are part of the whole game.

Colleges are clever enough to throw you a bone though and they allow you a certain number of credits to take whatever class you want to take, they like to call them "electives" because the college student can *elect* which class they'd like to fulfill these credits. Could you graduate a full semester early if the college didn't require electives? **Probably** but then the college would miss out on $30,000 and you'd miss out on four months of college life—the not studying part—which is basically a **Lose-Lose** situation for all involved so... electives.

Your choice of electives is the real test of just how smart you are. It's the secret measure of how much this college has taught you, how much you have absorbed, how much you have grown. Elective courses are on a scale of difficulty ranging from *breathing* to *neuroscience.* Here's the measure of intelligence... the **smart people** take *breathing* and the **dumb people** take *neuroscience.* Elective classes should be easy—they are explicitly supposed to raise your GPA out of the dumpster—this is an unspoken phenomenon that everyone knows. Just like everyone knows that if you are taking an elective that falls on the *not easy* end of the scale, you're only taking it for one reason. **Because your crush is in that class.**

Here's the thing, **dumbo,** your crush is probably in that class because it's required for his or her major not because he or she is also dumb and their crush is in that class too. Though could you imagine if that was the reason everyone was in that class? Just a bunch of dumbos sitting around staring at the person next to them while the professor spews some English words that sound like Japanese. That would be a real **kick in the pants.**

If you decide to take a class just because your crush is taking it in the hopes that he or she will ask you to be study partners and then blah, blah, blah, life, life, life, you're married with three kids, then you are way too dumb to be in the class.

Here is a list of ways that you can make this plan go horribly off the rails:

- Your crush is smart and knows all the answers but the professor calls on you and you stare at said professor, mouth agape, eyes glazed over because you don't even understand all of the words within the question.
- You work up the nerve to ask the crush what page you're supposed to turn to and you have spinach in your teeth.
- Your crush catches you trying to cheat off of him or her on a test because you're not smart enough to be there and they are, and they turn their test away from you—the horror!
- You finally get the seat next to your crush but you just ate a burrito and you pass gas...and everyone knows it's you.
- You drool while you're sleeping through class.

- Your sweater is on inside out.
- You only brush the front of your hair that you haven't washed in four days and your crush sits behind you.
- You run up to your crush after class and boldly ask if they want to study with you but you were sleeping for the last forty-five minutes and now have last nights faded bar stamp from the back of your hand on your cheek.
- You ask your crush to tutor you, cuz ya ballsy AF since you're still drunk from the night before, and he or she remarkably says yes because he or she is a good and charitable person and says they'll meet you in the library...and you have to ask where that is.
- And worst of all, you find out the day after add/drop day that the person who always seems to sit next to your crush is their long-term boyfriend or girlfriend that you didn't know existed. Son of a bitch!

Listen, we all have crushes, that's just a part of life and it's a great part. Crushes make you feel alive! But nothing will make you look worse than taking a class you shouldn't be in just to be near your crush. I mean committing a crime like **murder** would make you look worse and throwing up on your crushes shoes in a bar would too and also taking money from the tip jar on the counter of a Starbucks and stumbling out of your crushes best friend's room in the early morning wearing your underwear on the outside… ok there are a lot of things that would make you look worse but there's nothing that will make you look dumber. Ugh, crap, there are a lot of things that will make you look dumber, that's basically what this whole book is about, but you get the point, jeez! It's a waste of time and money and fun so take volleyball for an elective and meet your crush by bumping into them so randomly OMG in the dining hall OR at a bar like everyone else.

136:

Don't Think You Won't Hear Crazy College Stories From Every Adult Once You Start Freshman Year

Oh the grown-ups! One of the many college things that high school does not prepare you for– **besides almost everything**—is that the day you start school is officially the day that every person over the age of 35 thinks they can tell you, in uncomfortable detail, about all of the crazy shit they did when they were in college. There is a kinship that the over 35's feel with the newly minted college student. They've been patiently waiting for years to have someone new to *dust off* all their wild stories for.

You may do some **crazy** things but I promise you are not the first class of students to have done any of it. Do you think your dad's friend, the bald one with the belly that hangs over his pants, didn't win *Most Overnight Guests* for his dorm sophomore year? Totally did. Did you think that lady that taught your Sunday School class in third grade didn't do keg stands in the late eighties... in a dress? Yup, she did. Did you think your uncle didn't have a green mohawk and get fined for smoking pot in his dorm room with the door open on St. Patrick's Day, or that your aunt didn't wake up one morning on the front porch of the college president's house? Did it and did it. It's all been done before by people who are now corporate professionals and parents and law enforcement agents and spiritual leaders and doctors and life coaches and every other kind of adult that I don't feel like listing anymore. And they all want you to know about it.

You will likely start hearing these stories around Thanksgiving break freshman year. And then again at the next holiday party. You'll definitely hear them at receptions after funerals and weddings. Pretty much as soon as people are on their second drink, the sight of you all **pale and unhealthy** with straggly hair brings back memories and everyone now assumes that you are old enough to hear about those memories. Some of the stories will be funny, some a little uncomfortable, some slightly exaggerated as the over-35 is subconsciously challenging you to maintain their position as the leader on the craziness board so be prepared and just go with it. Hey, you never know, you might just get some ideas for things to do when your break is over, wink wink.

137:

Don't Poop
In The Street

I feel like I shouldn't *have* to say this but then again I feel like if I embraced that feeling then you would be looking at a bunch of blank pages right now. You know, like when you're looking at your Math 101 textbook. But when I read an article about people in a town in England being **all hot and bothered** because the college students were partying and then **pooping in the street** it suddenly became clear that perhaps there *are* college students out there that don't know that they shouldn't do this.

When you're drunk things loosen up a little bit. Your inhibitions loosen up. Maybe your moral compass loosens up. Sometimes your grasp of grammar might get a little loose. Perhaps your gag reflex does too. But one thing that should never loosen up is your **anal sphincter.** You should never allow yourself to get so drunk that you have to stop what you're doing and **shit right in the street.** Try to imagine the nickname you will never live down if you stumble out of a house party, drop your pants and crap in the street.

Here are a few possibilities:

- Street Shitter
- Party Pooper
- Doo Doo Debbie
- Doo Doo Danny
- The Mad Shitter
- Shit Demon
- Sir Shits A Lot
- Mayor of Shit Street
- Poo Poo Princess
- Crap Bandit
- Dingleberry Butt
- Loose Deuce
- Craptain
- And...Isn't that the one who shit in the street?

There may be many more possibilities and every one of them will stay with you for the rest of your life. But this one is about more than just the inevitable nickname, it's also because normal people live around **your shit,** people walk their dogs past **your shit,** they drive their cars over **your shit** and get **your shit** jammed into the grooves on their tires and then park **your shit** on their driveways where their children will sit while making chalk drawings. **It's freakin' gross.**

If you ate some bad tacos right before you went to a party and you suddenly have an emergency pooping situation then cut the line to the bathroom—nobody will remember the next day that you're the asshole that cut the line—if that's not possible then maybe run to the back of a garage where no one ever goes and let it out there but that's only in an emergency. **Listen,** if you have to go that bad then go outside, shit your pants, walk home, shower, throw your clothes in the garbage, get redressed and go back out, no one will even know you were gone. But if you shit in the street, people will know... for the rest of their lives. CLENCH YOUR BUTT CHEEKS, STREET SHITTER!

138:
Don't Go Surfing On The Top Of A Moving Vehicle

At some point decades ago, **wild dumb teen-agers** thought it would be cool to stand on the top of a car while it was moving and pretend that they were surfing. There are pictures of it online probably—most likely in black and white—and you might see someone doing it in a movie that was set in the 1970's or something like that. That person in the movie **probably dies** but that somehow doesn't stop dumbass college students from giving it a try.

The problem with this, though, is that decades ago when people first started doing it, the roofs of the cars were like eighteen feet wider and twenty inches thicker than on cars today. Hell, the streets were probably double the size, too. And, since the cars were so *goddamn big*, they only went like ten miles an hour maximum.

Today's cars are not the same cars that they had way back then. So car surfing back then was only semi-crazy. Today, it's a **literal death sentence.**

A few tidbits to consider here:

- If you stand on the roof of a car and it starts to dent- don't surf on it.
- I you can straddle the roof of a car—it's too small... and also you sound really flexible.
- If a car you're standing on turns on—jump off of it before it starts moving.
- If you don't want your friend, the driver, to be arrested for man-slaughter—don't stand on the freakin' roof.
- If you don't want to die—just avoid cars in college almost entirely (unless of course they're being driven by paid professionals then go for it, but sit in the car, not on it).

Let's just be crazy and assume that the purpose of a car is to transport people from one place to another and designed to do so where the car surrounds the bodies of the people not the other way around. Car surfing may be initially exhilarating but that high wears off pretty quickly when you're in a coma from the head injury that you sustain when you fall off the tiny car. A body cast is the car surfers equivalent to a **chastity belt**. Save the car surfing stories for the over forty crowd where at the conclusion of the story you can get all judgmental and discuss the health and safety ramifications of that life choice—mocking someone for car surfing is way less douchy than actually doing it and that's a situation that almost never happens.

139:

Don't Dance On A Bar

Dancing on a bar looks great in movies. In real life however, **it's a terrible idea**. First of all, if you are dancing on top of a bar that means you're drunk. There is no shot that you are confident enough while sober to publicly perform at that level. So knowing that you just had four Jaeger Bombs and three shots of tequila with gin and tonic chasers, you should also know that the bar you are about to climb up on has basically become a tight rope. Your depth perception is currently being **metabolized by your liver** and while your rhythm may suddenly be on *fire,* the dance moves you're about to try out are way too big for that dance floor tight rope designed to just hold a row of cups and maybe some elbows.

Let me paint this picture for you: You're drunk enough to be totally uninhibited but **not drunk enough to shit in the street,** you look amazing, your hair is working and your outfit doesn't have vomit on it yet. Everyone is in a great mood, three of the people that you want to hook up with are there, and the music is pumping. That's when you notice the bright gleaming bar surface and somehow it seems to be calling your name. Please note, the bar is *not* calling your name and it's bright and gleaming because it's waxed and covered in spilled booze—so basically it's a **wooden slip-n-slide.**

Your favorite song comes on and you just **lose it.** You scream for joy and assume that everyone else does too because your scream is loud enough to sound like a bar full of screams. You hand your drink to the person next to you, push your way through the row of people waiting for the bartender's attention and haul your big ass right on up—the stage is yours. What you don't see is the people looking at you like you're a piece of shit cause you just set back their chances of getting a drink by a good three minutes, which as we all know is a *month-and-a-half in drink wait time,* and you also don't see the bouncer getting up from the stool by the door and heading in your direction.

So you start dancing and laughing super hard cause this is your moment. You're having the time of your life and thinking that maybe you'll start a trend and other people will come join you and you're fine with that cause now this is a dance party. Then all of a sudden that tight rope starts to wobble, that slip-n-slide gets slipperier, your super fly dance move is just three inches too big, and you tumble head first off the side of bar and end up with your face in puddle of bar floor muck with your feet in the air. *Oh boy.* Somehow this great idea comes to a screeching halt and to make matters even worse, it's the bouncer—not one of your three prospective hook ups—that picks your drunk ass up. And then of course tosses your **drunk ass** onto the curb.

Here's the thing about bar dancing: it never looks like it does in the movies cause the actors in the movies aren't actually drunk—usually—and the bar surface is probably triple the size of a real bar and the people around the bar aren't really waiting for a drink and the dance is choreographed and practiced for seventeen hours and the actors never fall off. But in real life all of that is the opposite and the falling off part is basically guaranteed. So if you don't want your potential hook ups to know what your underwear looks like until you're actually hooking up, if you don't want to be banned from the bar that everyone goes to every week, if you don't want to end up with a torn meniscus, or if you don't want to end up with your face in a puddle of bar floor sludge then for the love of God, do *not* dance on a bar.

140:

Don't Put It In Your Mouth If You Don't Know Where It's Been

My friends, **this is a solid rule** that you should always adhere to. As a matter of fact maybe make it your mantra. Some people have mantras like: *I will be a good person* or *My body is my temple so I will take care of it* or *I will make a difference in the world* or *Today I will help someone in need*. Those mantras are great, but in college they can be hard to follow and you don't want to **disappoint yourself** when you fall off the mantra wagon. So my suggestion is to choose: *I will not put something in my mouth if I don't know where it's been* as your mantra. Hey man, **everyone has to stand for something** and I think this is good thing to stand for.

If you're unclear about things that you shouldn't put in your mouth, let me offer you some suggestions:

- The bottle of beer on the floor next to the couch that has cigarette butts in it
- The half-eaten slice of pizza on the steps outside your dorm
- A stranger's pee pee place
- The Chapstick you found on the sidewalk outside of a bar
- A toothbrush in the bathroom at someone else's house party
- Any of the red cups still on the table the morning after a night of Flip Cup ended
- The chewed up pen left on the desk from someone who was in the classroom before you
- The tap still attached to a keg lying on its side under a porch
- Any part of a police officer

If you choose to make this your mantra you will likely have an easier time avoiding things like hepatitis, meningitis, rabies and incarceration. These are all things you should try to avoid when you are in college, and also the rest of your life, but definitely in college. I should point out that none of the things on this list should really go in any other orifice of your body either but I'm not shooting for the moon here. Baby steps.

141:

Don't Think Your Music Tastes Won't Change When You Get To College

Colleges try to organize freshman roommates according to their similarities. They send out surveys asking you what your sleep and study habits are like, they ask what kind of food you eat, they ask about your fitness habits and your favorite this and that. They also ask what kind of music you listen to. I'm sure high school seniors are honest when they fill out these forms cause high schoolers are *always* honest. But somehow when you get to college and get ready to put on your classic rock playlist, your roommate beats you to it with some **hardcore death metal** with the bass turned up to ten. So the person across the hall turns up their *indie folk* to drown out your roommates bass and then the person three doors down goes rouge and cranks up the **country** even louder. When you wake up from your seizure you think, *shit it's gonna be a long year.*

Fear not because a person thinking their favorite genre is the best and everything else **totally blows** is just a first-day thing—maybe a first week thing. But pretty soon, you will realize that the music you swore you'd never listen to suddenly sounds fairly decent. You may even find yourself knowing the words to some songs from an alternate genre and then by the time you go home to your conservative small town for Thanksgiving break you have fully embraced the reggae lifestyle and even have a fresh Bob Marley tattoo on your shoulder to prove it. But ease up on the Jamaican accent cause **nobody's buying it, Daniel.**

Music is one of the coolest things ever; there is literally a genre for everyone and always that one song that sums up exactly how you feel at any given moment in your life. Decades after college ends, a song will come on the radio and bring you back to that one time in college when you... [*whatever awesome thing you did*]. Music unifies us, it articulates how we're feeling, it changes our moods, it enhances our experiences. So when you get to college have an open mind about the music that everyone around you is listening to. Experience something new, expand your musical pallet, but maybe **stay away from too much pan flute** cause that shit is annoying to everyone.

142:
Don't Think Having A Car In College Is So Great

Everybody knows the *grass* is always greener on the other side. And one of those greener grass sides rolls onto campus with your friend's sweet new ride at the beginning of junior year, by *new ride* of course I mean **1997 Chevy.** Most colleges don't allow freshmen to have cars so that's easy. You and all of your friends are in the same boat—which is not a car—you have to take the bus if you want to get someplace off campus, in other words you have to Uber everyplace you want to go. And it's fine, no one really cares cause you're more preoccupied by all of the **bad decisions** you're making to even think about a car. Then sophomore year comes and it's still fine cause most people still don't have car. But enter junior year and things start to change.

Suddenly some of your friends don't get dropped off by their parents at the beginning of the fall semester. Some of them actually drop themselves off. Because they got to campus on their own. In their own car. **What!?** Now your first thought may be—Damn it I wish I had a car.. *waa waa waa*. But that is often quickly replaced with—Oh sweet, my new best friend has a car.. wooooooo. And that's when being the person *with* the car becomes a real **pain in the ass.**

When you have a car guess what happens. Everyone suddenly needs to go out on a breakfast run or to the minimart that every college town seems to have (try finding a minimart in a non-college town—they don't exist). Guess who gets to pick up the kegs? Guess who has to drive their friends to the hospital *the next day*? Guess who has to pay for gas? Guess who has to **remember** to *get* gas? Guess who has to field constant requests to borrow said car? Guess who has to drop everyone off back home during Thanksgiving break? And, dare I say it, guess who just might have to be the designated driver?

Friends, having a car on campus is not all it's cracked up to be. As a matter of fact it may be more of a burden than a convenience. I'll tell you who it is great for though—it's great for the friends of the car owner because they get rides they don't have to pay for and they don't have to clean out the eight bags worth of fast food wrappers that somehow accumulate on one **super hungover Sunday morning**. Oh, and stay away from the person who rolls up to campus in a shiny, brand new, red BMW cause that person is **obviously a douchebag.**

143:

Don't Try To Bring Everything You Own To College

College and high school are **wildly different animals.** Just because they are both related to education doesn't mean they actually have anything in common. You can't even say that it's like comparing apples to oranges because at least those are both fruit. Think of it more like comparing **bricks to gorillas;** trust me that would be more realistic– and yes, *college* is the jungle animal in that comparison.

One of the things that's particularly different about high school and college is that you don't have an entire house or apartment or condo to keep all of your stuff in. You pretty much have a refrigerator-sized box to JAM everything into and that includes your bed, dresser, and desk. I know that packing can be hard, you have visions of wearing this outfit with those accessories and playing every sport you've ever heard of—*and some you haven't.*

You need thirty-seven throw pillows and super cool floor-length drapes so your room **reflects your personal style.**
You need lamps with special soft lighting and full-length mirrors. You need rugs. You need nineteen pairs of shoes *just in case.* You need everything that your local office supply store sells. You need, you need, you need. Well guess what, d-bag, you don't *need* and you can't *have* cause you have two roommates and all three of you have to fit yourselves and your shit in a room the size of a large dog crate.

People who come to campus with a full rental truck are people whose parents go home with an **almost full** rental truck. There is just no space for all of the stuff you think you need. And although the withdrawal you feel yourself suffering as your mini fridge and microwave head back home seems like it will never go away, trust me it will take you one day to get acclimated to being a minimalist like everyone else. You forget all about those throw pillows when you bring your first hook-up home. Those rugs would've been hard to clean the vomit out of. That special lamp would've gotten broken in your first room party. And you probably would've considered **smoking the drapes** when you ran out of pot. It's all better waiting for you back at home.

If you have one week's worth of outfits and a **month's worth of underwear** you'll be fine. If you have two towels and one set of sheets, you'll make it. If you have a couple of notebooks and some pens, that's probably good, or forget that and just rely on your laptop. **Slap some posters on the walls** and definitely bring a fan, your toothbrush, some toothpaste and deodorant. Then use whatever space you have left for *condoms and disinfecting* wipes and your room will have everything you actually need. So get used to scaling down, fancy pants, and lower your standards for how many times you can wear the same outfit. No one cares.

Oh, I should point out that if you think you're gonna beat the system by doing one of those things were you hoist your bed five feet up in the air and make a great "study nook" underneath it with cute twinkly lights and blankets and shit, make sure you add in an air mattress cause there will be a minimum of three nights each week that you'll be too inebriated to haul your ass up onto that skyscraper. Dial it back, Princess and the Pea, and "study" while you're sitting *on* your bed like the rest of us.

144:
Don't Fall Off The Porch At A House Party

There is just nothing quite like a **college house party.** I mean that literally, there is absolutely nothing like it. Maybe if you partied in an abandoned building that might be somewhat like it because in both situations there may be an odd chair on its side, vomit somewhere, a non-working toilet and possibly a homeless person. And in both situations there is the vague awareness that the cops might come and break it up. But other than an abandoned building party, there is definitely nothing like a college house party.

Once you graduate from college you will never again get to experience the **voracious need** to put your head through a wall and the **balls** to actually do it. After college, music at a party is played at a level that won't make your ears ring for the next seventeen months. When you go to a party after you graduate you actually have to throw up *IN* a toilet and that toilet is then expected to fully flush or, and this might seem crazy, not get drunk enough to throw up in the first place—why bother, I know.

College house parties are a unique and glorious experience, they are a rite of passage, an expectation, and something that colleges don't put on their brochures but we all know that's what pending students really want to know about. Have fun at the house parties you go to but there is one thing I must caution you about. Do not, under any circumstances, fall off the porch at a house party.

There are many reasons why you should avoid falling off a porch at a house party. Here are a few:

- Death
- Paralysis
- Broken bones
- Testicular explosion (I'm not sure about that one but hey, if you land the wrong way it could happen)
- Irrevocable dumbness
- Landing in dog shit
- Missing something great happening inside
- Having to wait in line again to get back in
- Landing in human shit
- Losing your buzz
- Losing your watch

Landing in urine

Being known as the person that fell off the porch

When college students are in the process of choosing which off-campus house they want to live in, it seems that **a porch trumps all other amenities**. The floors in the house all tilt to the left? Doesn't matter, there's a porch. There's only one shower but the landlord will rent the place out to fifteen people? Doesn't matter, there's a porch. There are three owl nests in one of the bedrooms? Doesn't matter, there's a porch. The stove is plugged into an extension cord meant to handle one strand of Christmas lights then snaked out the window and into the window of the house next door and plugged into an outlet inside their bathtub? Doesn't matter, there's a porch.

I get it, drinking beer out of a **red cup** on a porch rules, but when you finally make it to this version of nirvana (the existential place, not the band) please be cautious. Stay in the middle of the porch. Don't sit or stand on the railing. And if you're super drunk, just stay indoors where your chances of falling off the house are reduced by a good **33%**.

145:

Don't Die On Spring Break

It would be super easy to die on Spring Break. It's almost harder *not* to die than to actually die, but I feel like you can do it, if you can take the time to read this book then you can probably be smart enough to *not* die on Spring Break. Spring Break during college is the **stuff of legends.** There are movies made about it, there are music videos filmed during it, there are entire companies that actually employ real people totally dedicated to the college Spring Break phenomenon. And let me tell you, IT *IS* A PHENOMENON.

You have probably been aware of college Spring Breaks from the time you were in high school. And as each year of your life grew closer to those college years, your awareness grew. You started to imagine what it would be like. You pictured yourself on Spring Break. You picked out places you might like to go—Someplace, Mexico. And you were right to dream those dreams, because Spring Break is all that **and more.**

Spring Break is foam parties. It's pool volleyball. It's white sandy beaches filled with pale, doughy college bodies in bathing suits. It's losing your Juul in the ocean... or the sand...or a bush...or someone's bed...or behind a building...or at a club...or... psh, it's Spring Break, **you can't remember where you've been.** Spring Break is unlimited booze for the equivalent of six American dollars. It's hot tubs in your hotel room. It's glow stick bracelets. It's hooking up with strangers from other colleges. Spring Break is a non-stop party, morning, noon and night. Spring Break is the single-most **unhealthy** thing you will ever do in your entire life.

When you go on Spring Break, here are a few rules to keep in mind:

- Supplement your booze with the occasional bite of food. A pineapple wedge on the side of your basketball-sized cup of blue liquor doesn't count and just because your drinks are slushy doesn't make them food.
- Use the condoms that you brought with you and if you were super optimistic and brought twenty-five of them. Then do a public service and share them with your friends—don't be a hoarder, you're not gonna have sex twenty-five times, you porn star.
- Sleep for a few hours. This should be done in a bed, but it can be done

poolside. Although I would caution you to not sleep in the pool, which may seem reasonable after partying for thirty-two hours straight.

- Wear sunblock. Your vitamin D deprived body hasn't seen sunlight in six months and it's hard to rage on the dance floor with sun poisoning, and also no one wants to hook up with someone who looks like they maybe have leprosy.
- Don't wander away from the resort you're staying at, that's just basic common sense but you checked common sense with your luggage when you got on the plane, and it got lost in baggage claim—so stay at the resort.
- And, for the love of God, drink some water—actual bottled water, not pool, ocean or toilet water.

Spring Break is amazing but you will want to live to tell the tale. If you follow those few simple rules, it will make the odds of surviving Spring Break just slightly better. BTW, don't plan to do anything for the five days after you return from Spring Break because that's how long it will take you to recover. Woo! Party!

146:

Don't Be So Quick
To Get A Pet

Pets are great and college is also great but pets at college? Not so great. Pets love us and we love pets. Well if your pet is a cat then it probably doesn't love you, it thinks you're dumb and annoying. And if your pet is a gerbil or some other rodent then it also probably doesn't love you, it thinks you're a monster. But if your pet is a dog then it definitely loves you. So that's settled. Oh, and if your pet is a bird, screw you.

When you're at college you may think that getting a pet is a great idea. But let me assure you, it doesn't even make the list of *great ideas*, it actually finds itself pretty low on the list of *moderately fair ideas*. I know you had a pet at home and it was fun but what you didn't realize was that, believe it or not, pets cost money and require attention. You have to pay for food and maybe even vet bills. If it's a rodent of some kind (not the rats that burrowed their way in uninvited, feasting on that pizza you left on the floor, but a rodent that you purchase from a pet store), you will have to pay for a habitat and bedding. Pets expect some kind of human interaction, they may have to be taken **outside to poop and pee** even when it's raining and you're hung over. They can't get high with you and binge watch Netflix cause getting your pet high is illegal and **also awful** but if you get high and settle in for some binge watching your pet will probably suddenly have diarrhea in your room and that will ruin your morning. You can forget about going on a three-day bender, you won't even be able to go on a two-day bender, actually you won't even be able to pass out at someone else's house cause you have to take care of your pet.

Listen, I get it. We all think having a pet is awesome and it is, just not at college. Save the pets for after you graduate and get a job where you can actually afford one, and are sober enough to take care of it. Pets are a priority and at college, *you* are your only priority. Here's a small cautionary tale, one of my housemates found an adorable little abandoned puppy one night, so she took it home and let it sleep in her bed that night and when she woke up in the morning, her **bed was full of puppy shit and worms.** I think that's all I need to say about that.

147:

Don't Jump In A River In The Winter

Rivers are cool. As far as bodies of water go, rivers probably rank third—behind oceans and bays but definitely ahead of lakes (Great Lakes excluded cause they're pretty much small oceans) and I won't even mention ponds because those are basically **nature's toilets.** Rivers are great for white water rafting or canoeing or fly-fishing or some other activity you won't do during college. They make a nice background for pictures and are cool to look at when you're high. But rivers are warm weather places and should be avoided at all costs during the cold winter months.

When you're in college, **alcohol is one of your five main food groups.** Alcohol is aggressive so it probably bumps those pansy-ass vegetables right off the food pyramid and then gets its swagger on and plows through all the way to the top. So let's say that, at some point during college, alcohol will be your number one food group. It is around this time that you will be at a bar that happens to be situated either right next to, right on, or pretty near a river and it will be cold as hell outside And when you find yourself in this **Bermuda Triangle of alcohol, river and freezing-ness** you will likely think it's a great idea to jump into the river. Well, I hate to break it to you, **schmuck-o**, it's actually a terrible idea.

Here's what will definitely happen if you jump into a river while drunk during the winter:

- Your beer jacket will be rendered totally useless immediately upon contact with the freezing water
- You won't be able to get back inside the hot, sweaty bar
- Your balls will end up in your esophagus
- Your nipples will become a lethal weapon and you will be charged with a Class B felony for having them
- Your Uber will show up and then drive away without you cause you're soaking wet and beginning to freeze up and still charge you
- You will be instantly sober
- Your night will end way too early
- You'll get pneumonia and won't be able to drink for the next 72 hours

- You'll lose your phone and your wallet
- And you'll probably get molested by some three-eyed creature lurking below the surface of said river just waiting for the next dumb college student to make a bad decision

Listen, let's get real. If you do jump in a river in the winter you will probably achieve some level of **legendary status**. People will remember that you did it and will remember you fondly even while recognizing what a **complete dumbass** you are. But, when you see your mom a couple of weeks later and you haven't totally thawed out yet and she, in an act of motherly concern, notices two lumps in your throat and instinctively massages them thinking your lymph nodes are swollen, she will actually be massaging your nuts. **And that is goddam unthinkable.** So leave the river excursions for Spring Weekend and save everyone in your family from years of therapy.

148:
Don't Think That The Good Life Ends At Graduation

Everyone that goes to college is told this same sentence: *Enjoy it, it's the best four years of your life.* In some ways that sentence is probably true, but I think it's a little misleading. That sentence, which I like to think is said to encourage college freshmen and maybe make them less nervous and more excited, is a little conflicting because college students remember it and it makes graduation harder than people realize. College graduation is a bitter-sweet experience. On some level you're ready and excited for what comes next but on another level you're sad to leave this completely outrageous life that you created for yourself over the past four years.

College is amazing because for the first time in your young life you don't really have to answer to anyone. You don't have a curfew, no one is telling you to eat your vegetables, you don't have to pretend you're sober or asexual. You make your own decisions. You aren't told what is right and what is wrong, you finally get to figure that out on your own. You make mistakes and do dumb things but you also make good decisions and do great things, all by yourself. It is a wild and remarkable time and I hope that when it's over, you will be able to look back on it and be happy. I hope that you will be that over-thirty-five-year-old who burdens the next generation of college students with your inappropriate stories. But I hope that you *don't* think that the good life ends at graduation because, my friends, it just doesn't.

College is amazing because of all the new things you get to experience, but when college is over you still get to experience new things. Your first job, your first apartment, your first marriage... for 50% of you. And there are things that happen after college that are so profound they make you see life in a completely different way. You may find yourself making a real difference in the world by helping people, putting other people's needs before your own. You may rise up to a level in business that even you didn't think possible. You may write a book that makes people laugh and remember the crazy things that they did *that one time*. You may have a child that simply takes your breath away every time you look at him.

The good life doesn't end when you graduate from college. No, the reality is, that's when the good life is just getting started. So have fun in college. Be free, be wild, laugh a lot, be a good friend, own your mistakes and your achievements and when you're finished you will be ready to have a great and meaningful life. When you start college, know that you are embarking on a wild four years and then four short years later the most amazing things will start to happen. Whichever way you look at college, *it's only four years.*

Peace out.

Top Ten Lists!

Hey man, I know reading all of these super high level *Don'ts* probably exhausted you so I condensed some tips down even further into top ten lists. Lists unburdened by excess words like *unburdened*. Think of them as a quick and handy reference guide for when you're too busy to read all fifteen words of one of the previous chapters.

TOP 10 THINGS TO LEARN:

1. How to use a condom
2. How to tap a keg
3. How to cram for a test
4. How to get dressed in the dark
5. How to find your underwear under someone else's sheets
6. How to save all your spare change for $1 slices
7. The shortest route to the liquor store
8. The shortest route to the infirmary
9. How to write a paper
10. Sleeping rituals to drown out the noises of your roommate and their guest making baby animal noises at 3am

TOP 10 THINGS TO HAVE IN YOUR DORM ROOM:

1. Value-pack of condoms
2. Disinfecting wipes
3. This book
4. Eye drops (for your "allergies")
5. Paper towels
6. Vomit receptacle
7. Speakers
8. Lights to illegally string around the top of the wall
9. Life Alert (at least seniors don't need an excuse, you're just a drunken dumbass)
10. A pad of blank doctor's notes you stole off of his desk

TOP 10 THINGS TO BRING
ON SPRING BREAK:

1. Condoms
2. Money for sunblock (because you were too busy buying your condoms to remember SPF)
3. Bathing suit
4. Clothing besides your slutty bathing suit
5. Your fake ID
6. Your douchey reflective color lens Ray-Ban aviators
7. The ability to forget a questionable decision
8. Water bottles (unless you want Montezuma's Revenge)
9. Money to bail your friend out of a Mexican prison
10. A ready, willing, and able liver

TOP 10 THINGS TO DO AFTER YOU GET BACK FROM SPRING BREAK:

1. Sleep
2. Get a full STD work-up plan
3. Drink tons of water
4. Take antibiotics
5. Eat several solid meals
6. Take multiple showers
7. Your homework (LOL funny right?)
8. Delete any spring break pics you posted on social media
9. Make a list of things you'll never do again and then burn that list because there's another spring break one short year away
10. Pray for forgiveness

TOP 10 THINGS TO DO
ON A RAINY DAY:

1. Drink
2. Nap (because I'm sure you don't do enough of that already)
3. Clean your room
4. Watch an entire TV series on Netflix
5. Create a life plan and then abandon it
6. Play eight straight hours of video games
7. Shower
8. Call your parents… remember them?
9. Homework
10. Nothing

TOP 10 THINGS YOU NEED
FOR A HANGOVER:

1. A bed (anyone's will suffice)
2. A sexual romp (anyone will suffice)
3. Netflix
4. Water
5. Aspirin
6. Gatorade
7. A greasy meal
8. Pedialyte already on hand in your refrigerator
9. A shower
10. More alcohol

TOP 10 LAWS COLLEGE STUDENTS WILL PROBABLY BREAK:

1. Underage drinking
2. Public intoxication
3. Underage smoking a lot of things
4. Public urination
5. Trespassing
6. Public indecency (yeah I'm talking to you)
7. Vandalism
8. Breaking and entering
9. Publicly having sex
10. Publicly being a douchebag

TOP 10 THINGS TO DO
WITH THIS BOOK:

1. Read it
2. Worship it
3. Use it as a coaster
4. Use it to swat away a bee
5. Use it to waft your roommate's beer farts in the opposite direction
6. Decorate your coffee table with
7. Use it to wipe snow off your windshield
8. Walk around with it so people think you're smart because you have a book but also funny because it's THIS book
9. Wave a large bong hit away from a smoke detector with it
10. Horrify your parents (no matter how old you are) by putting check marks next to the things you've done

Acknowledgements

Charlotte, Nicole, Cassandra, and Ethan, my loves this book would not be nearly as dope without all you did to help create it. I thank you for your edits, your comments, your enthusiasm, your ideas, your energy, and your support. Though I recognize that since you are not editing this part there will probably be some ~~mistaes misties mistids~~ mistakes but hopefully you'll get the meaning. I value all you have done and all that you are. I am blessed to have you on this journey with me and am so grateful to know you.

Mom and Dad, thank you for sending me to college...and letting me stay all four years. I can't imagine a better way to spend all that tuition money, I mean besides a million better ways but none of them would have resulted in a book years later. Eh, maybe they would have but it definitely wouldn't have been this book. ;)

Beloved, everything is always for you. Thank you for sharing your stories and listening to mine, something about apples and trees. You are and always will be my inspiration for all that I do.